How Ludwig Guttmann Created the Paralympic Games

A SPORTING CHANCE

How Ludwig Guttmann Created the Paralympic Games

A SPORTING CHANCE

Lori Alexander

Illustrated by

Allan Drummond

HOUGHTON MIFFLIN HARCOURT

BOSTON NEW YORK

hmhbooks.com

The text was set in Adobe Caslon Pro.

Library of Congress Cataloging-in-Publication Data
Names: Alexander, Lori, author. | Drummond, Allan, illustrator.
Title: A sporting chance : how Ludwig Guttmann created the Paralympic Games / Lori Alexander ; illustrated by Allan Drummond.
Description: Boston : Houghton Mifflin Harcourt, [2020] | Audience: Ages: 7 to 10. | Audience: Grades: 4 to 6. | Includes bibliographical references and index.
Identifiers: LCCN 2019007462 | ISBN 9781328580795 (hardcover : alk. paper)
Subjects: LCSH: Paralympic Games--History--Juvenile literature. | Guttmann, Ludwig, 1899-1980--Juvenile literature. | Neurologists--Great Britain--Biography--Juvenile literature. | Jews, German--Great Britain--Biography--Juvenile literature.
Classification: LCC GV722.5.P37 A54 2020 | DDC 796.04/56--dc23
LC record available at https://lccn.loc.gov/2019007462

Manufactured in Malaysia
TWP 10 9 8 7 6 5 4 3 2 1
4500788129

For Lou and Kathy, my gold medal parents.
And for Nora and Dr. Francisco Valencia, my inspirations for this story.
— L. A.

For my wife, Gaye
— A. D.

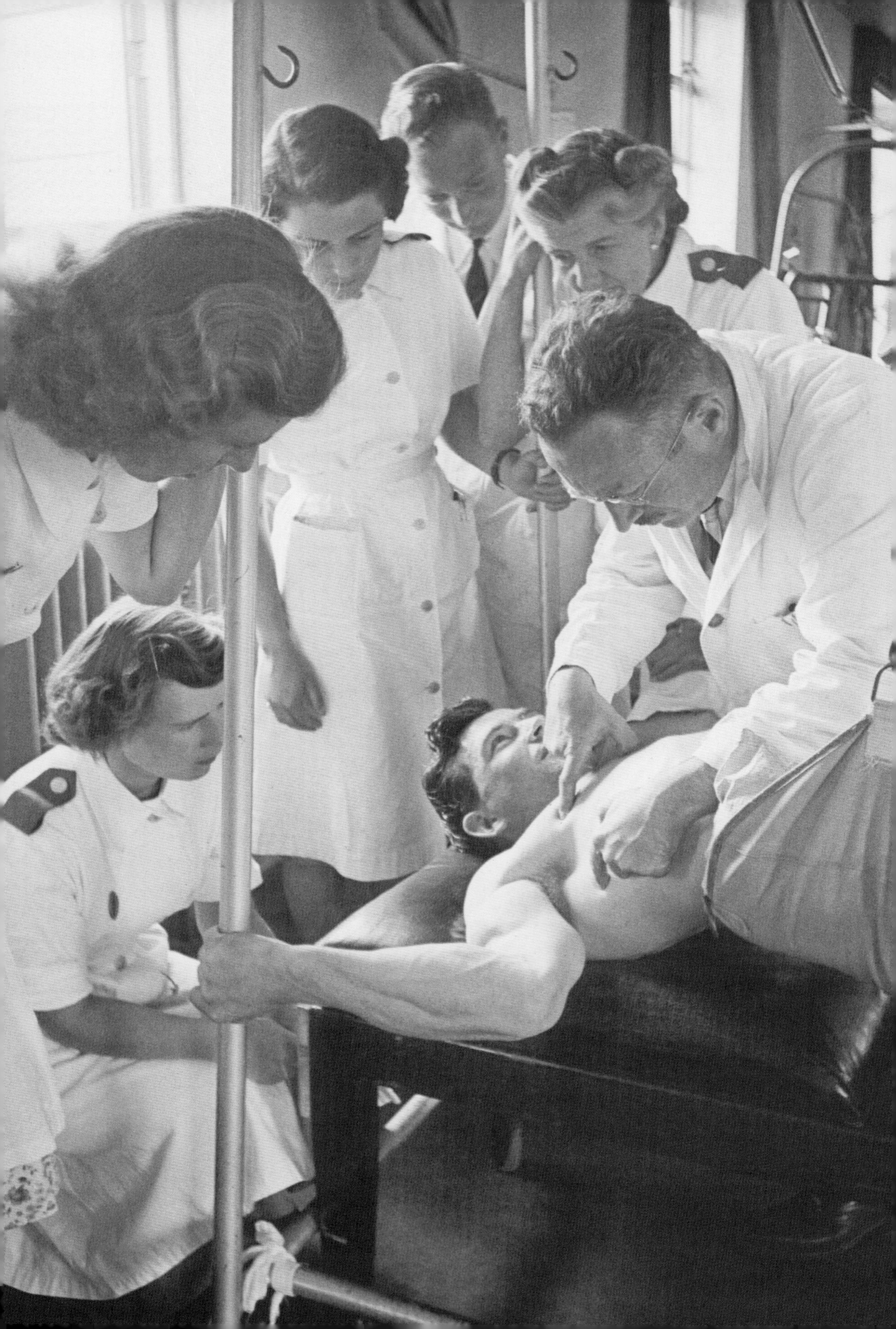

CONTENTS

Sport has played a very important part in the physical, psychological as well as social rehabilitation of the paralysed, and the profound value of sport in preventing these patients from retiring into inactivity cannot be exaggerated.

—*Dr. Ludwig Guttmann*

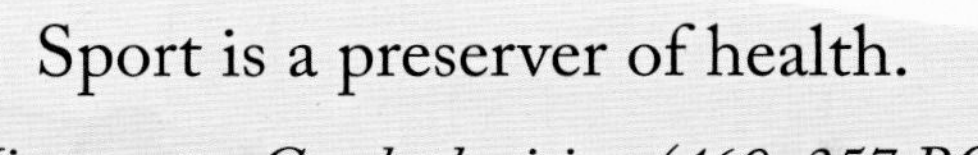

Sport is a preserver of health.

—Hippocrates, Greek physician (460–357 BCE)

Anyone who lives a sedentary life and does not exercise . . . even if he eats good foods and takes care of himself according to proper medical principles—all his days will be painful ones and his strength will wane.

—Maimonides, Jewish philosopher and physician (1135–1204)

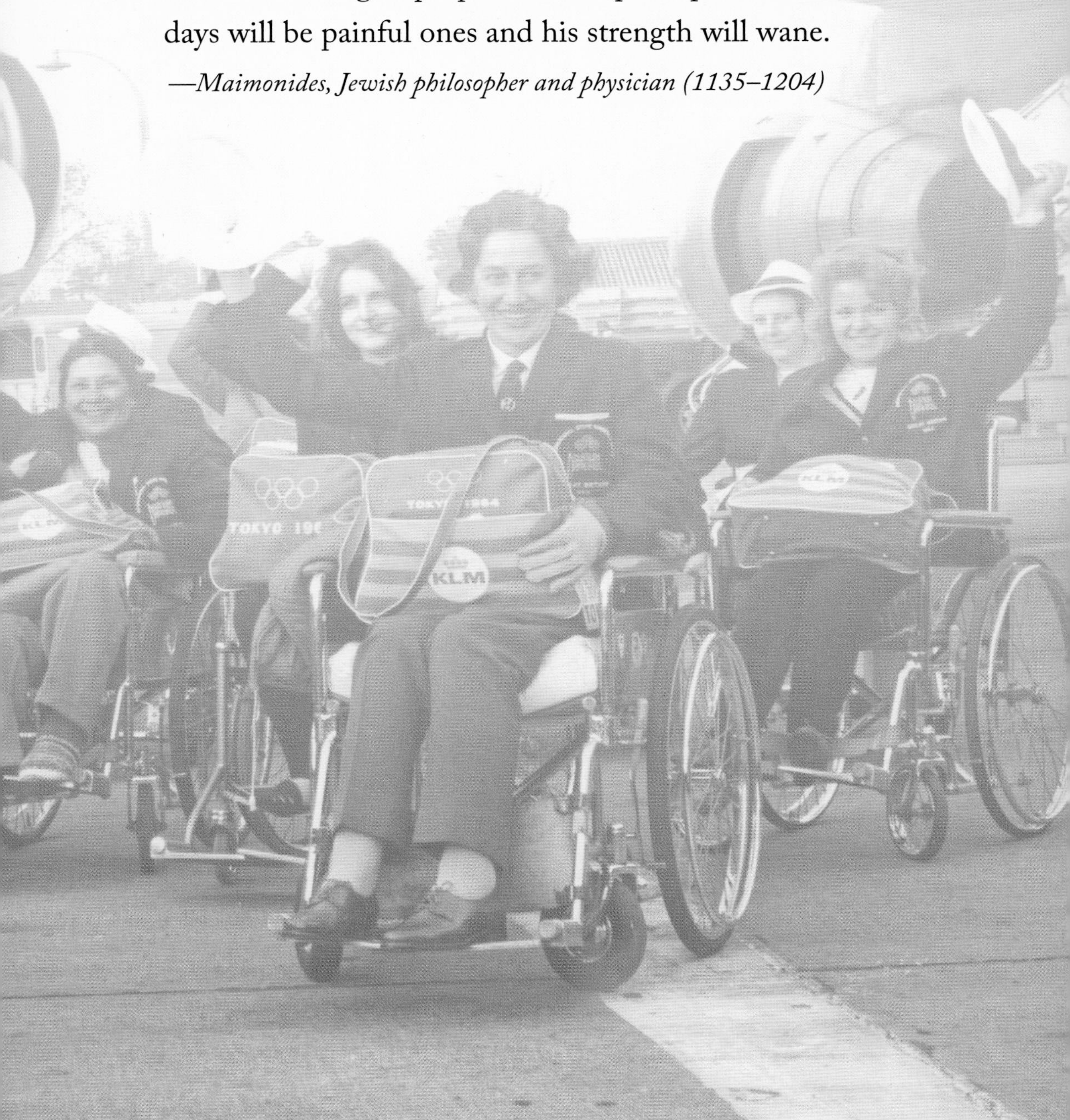

How Ludwig Guttmann Created the Paralympic Games

A SPORTING CHANCE

Chapter 1

AN AILMENT NOT TO BE TREATED

In June 1944, Reg Townsend was digging a trench in the north of France when he heard an explosion. He shouted to his fellow soldiers to take cover in the six-foot-deep hole. But it was too late. Shrapnel rained from a second round of German mortar bombs. A nearby soldier was struck in the head. Reg was hit elsewhere: "I had the immediate sensation of floating in the air—most peculiar—but when I tried to move and found that I couldn't, I knew that I caught it in the spine."

Diagnosis

Paraplegia [pear-uh-PLEE-jee-uh] is a medical term used to describe a person who no longer has feeling in the legs and lower half of the body. This loss of feeling, also known as *paralysis,* may be caused by disease, stroke, or an accident in which the bones in the spine are fractured, dislocated, crushed, or compressed. Some common causes of spinal cord injury are car or motorcycle crashes, falls, gunshot or knife wounds, high-impact sports accidents, and diving into shallow water.

Wounded soldiers evacuated
by jeep; France, 1944

A page from the ancient Egyptian medical text in which the oldest known description of paraplegia is found

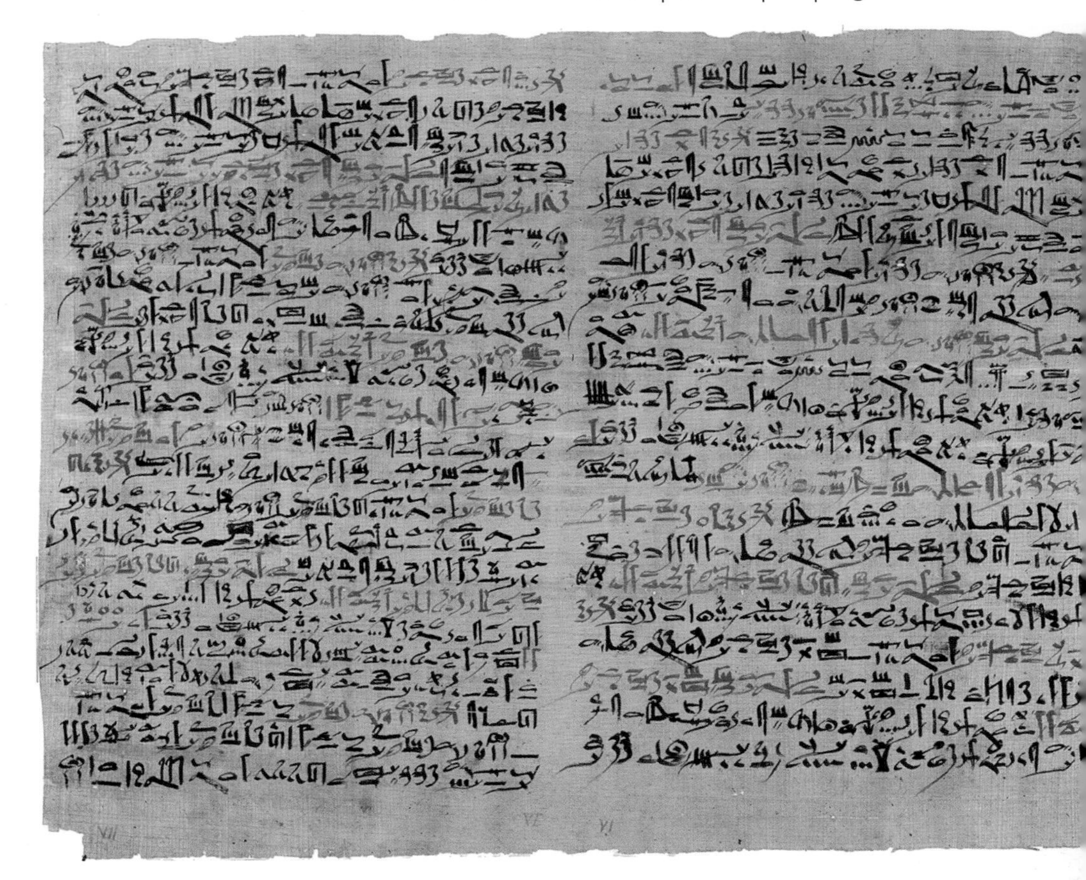

Reg Townsend was rushed from the battlefield to the base hospital. Within days, he was flown back to his home country of England, where doctors informed him that he had paraplegia and would never walk again.

The oldest known description of paraplegia was found on an Egyptian scroll dating back to the time of the Pyramids, around 2700 BCE. The scroll contained detailed medical instructions for treating forty-eight illnesses. But spinal injury was classified as simply "an ailment not to be treated."

Many years later, around 200 CE, a Greek surgeon named Galen studied the injuries of gladiators who had fallen from their chariots, possibly the earliest type of vehicle accident.

He learned that injuries near the top of the spine were the most serious and often led to death. Damage lower down the spine affected breathing, movement of the arms and legs, and control of the bladder and bowel. Damage to the lowest section of the spine might affect only the legs and bladder.

Over time, doctors and scientists learned more about the functions of the spine. Yet little was being done to help patients with spinal cord damage. Most died soon after their injury. In the 1940s, paraplegia was still considered by most "an ailment not to be treated."

Reg Townsend was cast in white plaster from neck to ankles. He spent his days flat on his back in a hospital bed, hidden away from other patients, cut off from the world.

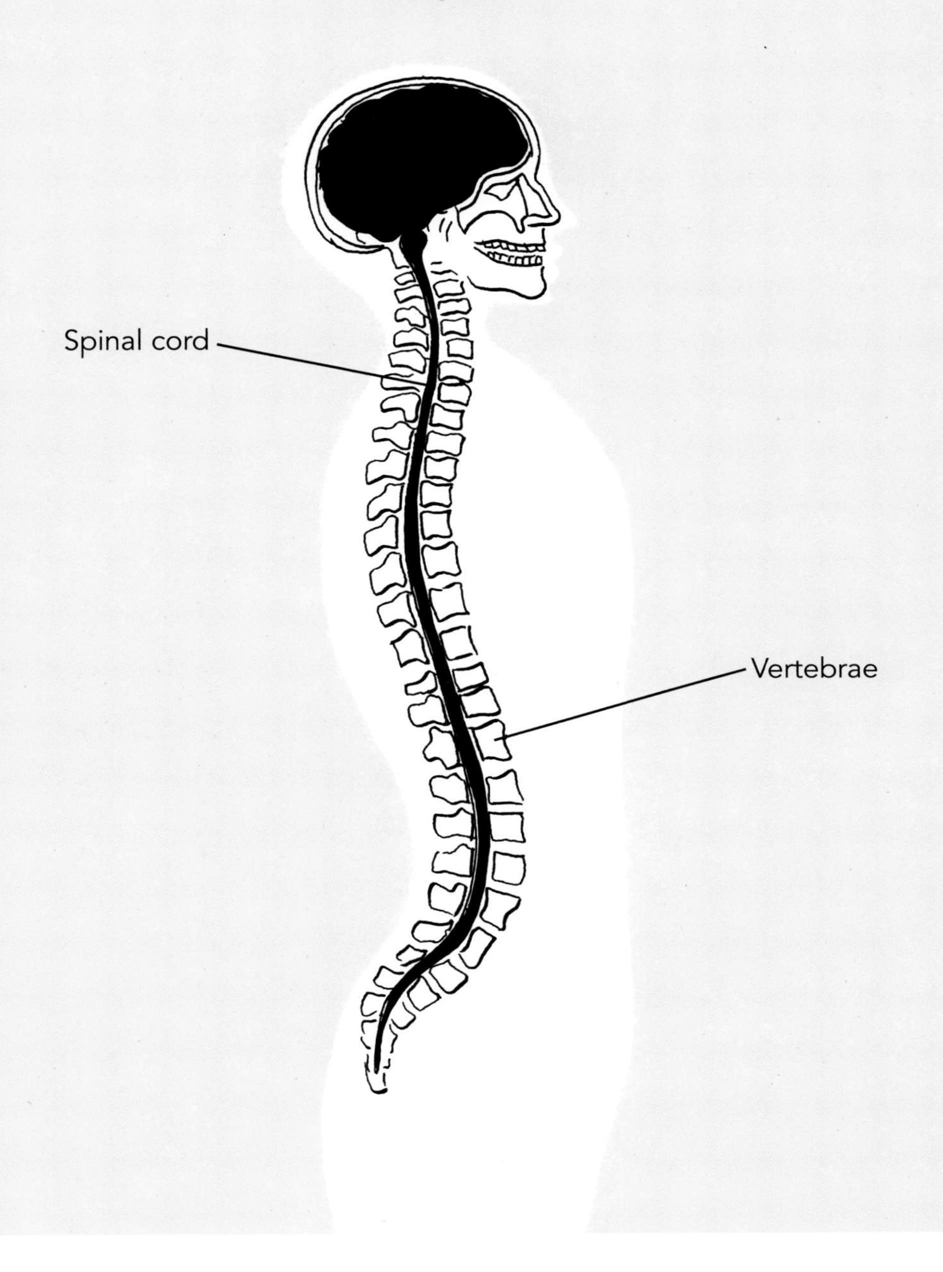
The Spine
Spinal cord
Vertebrae

Doctors had no hope for his recovery. They gave Reg, and others like him, an unfortunate nickname: “incurables.”

Could any doctor make a difference to these patients?

Chapter 2

HEADSTRONG

As a young boy, Ludwig Guttmann lived in a German mining town called Königshütte, near the border of what is now Poland. His father, Bernhard, ran a distillery business, while his mother, Dorothea, stayed busy raising Ludwig and his three younger sisters. Both of Ludwig's grandfathers owned farms. During the summers, Ludwig spent long days in the fields helping with the corn harvest.

When it came to school, Ludwig was less interested in hard work. He liked to do things his own way. So he put off

homework and projects until the end of each semester and then hurried to catch up and complete his assignments. He did not want to fail and repeat the dull classes! There were a few exceptions. Ludwig enjoyed learning about history. He liked singing with the school choir. Most of all, Ludwig was interested in sports. Running and soccer were his favorites. He was one of the shortest in his class, but he was fast. He outraced opponents. He flew across finish lines. Ludwig loved to win and made many friends among his teammates.

As a young Jewish boy, Ludwig faced other types of rivalries at school. One day at recess, a classmate of Ludwig's insulted another boy, calling him "a damned Jew." Ludwig stood up for his friend. He confronted the bully. When

Ludwig demanded an explanation for the name calling, the boy only yanked on Ludwig's tie, a special gift from his mother. A fistfight broke out. Before a teacher could stop the scuffle, the bell rang and the boys trudged back to class. Ludwig was let off with a warning. But the other boy received detention for the name calling. He had to apologize to both Ludwig and his Jewish classmate.

Little did Ludwig know, this type of anti-Semitic behavior—prejudice or aggression toward Jewish people—would become more frequent in Germany, and more dangerous, in the coming years.

Chapter 3

THE MINER

As Ludwig reached his final months of high school in early 1917, he was presented with an opportunity: He could take his final exams now and graduate early as long as he agreed to join the National Emergency Services. This organization placed volunteers in jobs where there were not enough workers. Still uninspired by his classes, Ludwig jumped at the chance to be done with school. Germany was facing its third year of war with Russia, France, and Britain. The Great War, later renamed World War I, affected many men in Ludwig's family. His father and several cousins served in the German armed forces. Ludwig was a healthy eighteen-year-old male. He too wanted to serve his country. While he waited to be called to duty, he passed his finals, finished school, and began his volunteer service.

With more than ten million German men engaged in the war, there were shortages of workers at the mines, the iron foundries, the hospitals, and the schools. Ludwig had some interest in medicine, so he was assigned the position of orderly at a local hospital. He moved patients from one part of the hospital to another, emptied bedpans, cleaned rooms, and changed sheets. When he was asked to hold up lights

German soldiers marching in World War I, circa 1916

German coal miners
in the early 1900s

for a surgeon to better see inside a patient, Ludwig's stomach churned. He rushed from the operating room, later confessing "I can't look at blood." It took several attempts before he could watch an entire operation.

The hospital was located in the middle of Königshütte's industrial area. Many of the patients were coal miners who had been injured at work. Mining jobs were dangerous from the start, but because of the war, the mines were now understaffed and accidents were even more common.

Ludwig assisted many patients during his time as an orderly. One was a young coal miner, not much older than

Ludwig himself. The miner was brought to the hospital with a broken back. He couldn't feel or move his legs. Ludwig read the notes in the chart: *complete paraplegia from the waist down.* The patient was hoisted up and away from his bed by four strong men so the doctor could work from underneath, attempting to realign the bones in the miner's fractured spine. Then the patient was cast in plaster from shoulders to ankles and left alone in a corner of the hospital, screened off from other patients.

Ludwig asked about the next steps for the young miner's recovery. But sadly, there were none. "Dead in six weeks at the latest," said one of the doctors. "Just watch him—you will see and learn."

Over the next month, the miner's eyes grew sunken. His face withered. He couldn't feel his bladder, so urine would

not empty properly. The bladder became infected with bacteria. He couldn't roll over because of the bulky cast. His weight pressed down on his backside. Skin is not meant to be pressed continuously in the same spots. Normally, a body is in motion, even during sleep, tossing and turning. Red, open sores formed along the miner's back where there was pressure from the mattress. Some of the wounds grew so deep, muscle and bone were exposed. These bedsores became infected as well. The infection spread. Only five weeks after his injury, the patient died, just as the doctor had predicted. The image of the young miner was one Ludwig would never forget.

It wasn't easy to avoid illness while working at the hospital. One afternoon Ludwig scribbled notes into a sick soldier's chart when he was showered by the man's coughs. Before long, Ludwig came down with a fever and sore throat. Weeks went by and Ludwig wasn't feeling any better. A lump appeared on the right side of his neck. When a doctor spotted it, Ludwig was rushed into surgery. A small glass tube was placed in his neck to drain the swelling. Later the tube was removed. But Ludwig's fever returned. The doctors decided the tube must remain in Ludwig's neck for a bit longer. They allowed him to continue his work at the hospital while he healed.

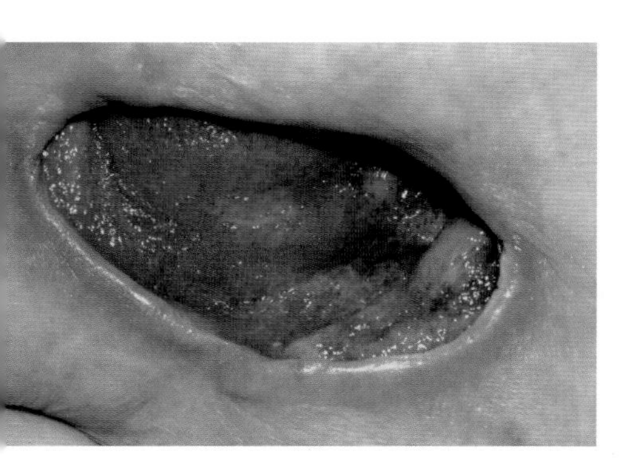

A bedsore on the lower back

In November 1917, Ludwig's days of volunteering came to an end. He

received papers calling him up to begin fighting in the war. But when Ludwig reported for duty, the inspecting officer saw the bandage on his neck. And when he heard about the glass drainage tube underneath, he excused Ludwig from duty and sent him home. "We have enough cripples here!" said the officer. Ludwig was disappointed. "War disabled, without having worn a uniform," he said to himself. Ludwig came from a patriotic family with many members serving in the German Army. He wanted to do something for his country. He wanted to make a difference too.

Chapter 4

A RETURN TO MEDICINE

With no chance to serve in the military, Ludwig decided to enter the University of Breslau to study medicine. He attended challenging classes in grand halls, taught by distinguished professors. Ludwig excelled. The months he spent volunteering at the hospital had prepared him well for medical school.

In addition to his studies, Ludwig found time for sports. He joined a group of Jewish students who formed a fencing club. The duels with classmates were intense and required a great deal of skill and concentration. In one competition

Ludwig attempted a new move. But he left his face exposed. His opponent's rapier blade struck Ludwig's left cheek, leaving a long cut. Thirteen stitches were required at once, without any anesthetic to numb the area. Instead, a friend pushed his thumbs into Ludwig's ears, in hopes that this action would take his mind off the pain. In spite of the injury, fencing remained Ludwig's favorite sport, and he proudly wore his "scars of honor." Participation in the Jewish club gave Ludwig and his teammates confidence, proving they were as good as any non-Jewish team.

Over the next several years Ludwig completed his studies and passed his medical school exams. He also spent time

University of Breslau, renamed University of Wroclaw in 1945, as it looks today

Feldberg, the highest mountain in the Black Forest, Germany

with his girlfriend, Else Samuel. They enjoyed hiking in the local Black Forest mountains. Ludwig had loved this place since he was a young boy, camping here with his scout troop. When he learned that young Jewish children were no longer allowed to join German scouting groups, he and a friend from medical school began a youth group of their own. They took boys and girls, ages six to seventeen, on weekend camping trips in the woods. They sang and cooked and slept under the stars. Else helped too.

For Ludwig's parents the scene was less tranquil. Germany had lost the war. The government signed an official document, the Treaty of Versailles, which required Germany to accept responsibility for the losses and damage of the war. Borders were redrawn, as the country had lost over 10 percent of its land. Also, Germany had to pay an enormous sum of money to Allied countries for the wrong and injury that Germany caused (the equivalent of more than $400 billion today). This had a disastrous effect on the country's economy. Inflation caused the German mark to lose value day by day, until the money was practically worthless. Many families sold their homes, businesses, and personal goods to make ends meet. Ludwig could no longer depend on money from his father. It was time to get a job.

Inflation in Germany after World War I. Thousands upon thousands of marks are worth less than a single American dollar, 1920s.

Since Ludwig enjoyed working with the children in the Jewish scouting organization, he decided to specialize in pediatrics. But in his interview he learned that there were too many children's doctors already. A friend told him of an opening in the department of neurology at a nearby hospital. Did Ludwig want a job working with

Ludwig's university identification card

brains, nerves, and spines? He remembered the young coal miner with the broken spine and the lack of treatment options. Could Ludwig make a difference? He interviewed for the job. And in October 1923 he began training with the accomplished neurosurgeon Dr. Otfrid Foerster.

Chapter 5

GROWING TENSION

Dr. Foerster was a strict boss. He worked eighteen hours a day, conducting research, performing surgeries, and seeing patients, both at the hospital and in his own home. Ludwig had to work long days too. He helped with research, assisted with surgeries, and carefully tracked the health status of each patient. Dr. Foerster was known to call the hospital late at night asking for updates. But Ludwig was learning from one of the best. Doctors from all over the world visited this neurology department to study Dr. Foerster's techniques.

After nearly five years, Ludwig's training was complete. In March 1928, at the age of twenty-eight, he was offered a prestigious job at a hospital in Hamburg, a port city in the north of Germany. Ludwig was excited by the new challenge: he would start his own neurology unit at a large university hospital. He and Else, who was now his wife, settled into their lives in the big city, about four hundred miles from Breslau.

Not long after his move, Ludwig received an urgent letter from his old boss, Dr. Foerster. His main assistant had died unexpectedly. Dr. Foerster asked Ludwig to come back and

fill the position. Ludwig enjoyed the fast pace and responsibility of running his own department in Hamburg. The decision was difficult. But in the end Ludwig was loyal to his mentor. He and Else moved back to Breslau. This time he worked with Dr. Foerster as an equal, not as a student. Over the next several years, Ludwig's reputation as a skilled surgeon grew. His family grew too. A son, Dennis, was born in 1929. Four years later came his daughter, Eva. Ludwig's future looked bright.

One starry evening, in late March 1933, Ludwig and Else strolled home from the cinema. They bumped into a doctor friend of Ludwig's. The man's face was filled with worry. He talked a mile a minute. The news was bad: Jewish doctors were no longer allowed to work in public hospitals. Ludwig could not believe what he was hearing. It must be a mistake. But within days, he received an official letter from the German government. He had been fired from his position in the neurology department. Even though Ludwig was one of the best surgeons in Europe, he was no longer allowed to treat non-Jewish patients. Dr. Foerster was distraught over the loss of his star pupil and friend, but there was little he could do.

A new government, the Nazi Party, had taken over Germany. Its leader, Adolf Hitler, was a persuasive speaker. He held massive rallies and gave rousing speeches to hundreds

Adolf Hitler speaking
at a Nazi rally, 1933

of thousands of German citizens. Hitler falsely blamed the Jewish people for the loss of the war and the difficult economic times that followed. He spread hateful propaganda in the form of a plan to make Germany strong again. His plan included ridding the country of all Jewish people, people of color, people with disabilities, lesbians and gay men, and other groups with non-German heritage. Hitler believed these individuals were inferior, and they would not be part of his strategy to build a "master race."

Street sign in Germany reads "Jews are not wanted here," circa 1936

Hitler created restrictive laws that limited individual freedoms. The laws prohibited Jewish people from holding government jobs; no longer could they work as teachers, professors, lawyers, police officers, newspaper journalists, or military personnel. Hitler encouraged German citizens to stop shopping in Jewish-owned stores. He instructed states to burn all books written by Jewish authors. Other policies limited the number of Jewish children allowed to attend public schools. Medical licenses were taken from Jewish

physicians and surgeons. They were no longer allowed to be called doctors; they were now *Judenbehandler*, "Jew treaters."

Many Jewish families decided it was safer to leave Germany. But Ludwig resisted the idea of leaving his country. He loved the beautiful mountains, the bustling cities rich with culture, his comfortable home filled with family and friends. He had worked hard to become a well-respected doctor in his community. Ludwig hoped the political unrest

Book burning in Germany, 1933

would pass within a few years. He got a new job as the head of neurology at an all-Jewish hospital in Breslau. Within five years, he was promoted to director of the entire hospital. But soon Ludwig's plan to wait out the cruel practices of the Nazi Party proved impossible.

Chapter 6

NIGHT OF BROKEN GLASS

On November 9, 1938, government officials called for the destruction of Jewish properties across Germany. Rioters hurled bricks through shop windows. They stole what they liked and destroyed the rest. Before setting fire to synagogues, they smashed stained glass and slashed sacred scrolls. They vandalized Jewish schools and cemeteries. Men in brown uniforms, Hitler's soldiers, banged on doors and entered Jewish homes, breaking furniture, taking valuables, and arresting husbands and fathers. Local police, firefighters, and

German citizens watched the acts of violence, but most were too afraid to help their neighbors.

Nearly one hundred Jews were killed and thirty thousand more were taken from their homes and placed in prisons and forced labor camps. The organized attacks, which lasted all day and into the night, were later named *Kristallnacht*, "the Night of Broken Glass."

Germans pass by the shattered windows of a Jewish-owned shop, 1938

Ludwig was on his way to work when he saw a beautiful seventy-year-old synagogue wrapped in flames and smoke. Soldiers kicked Jewish prayer books through the streets while the local rabbi was forced to watch. Ludwig was sickened by the sight. At the hospital, he instructed his staff to allow any male to be admitted without question. Ludwig wanted his hospital to be a safe place for Jewish refugees. Sixty-four men sought protection there on Kristallnacht.

The next morning, when Ludwig arrived at work, two Gestapo officers, members of the Nazi Party's secret police force, were waiting. They tapped their guns on Ludwig's desk, furious at him for hiding healthy Jewish men in hospital beds. "How can you explain this?" one shouted. Ludwig's heart raced. But he calmly escorted the officers from room to room. A stroke patient, who was paralyzed on his right side, groaned. Ludwig lifted the man's right arm and let it flop limply back onto the bed. "I take it you are satisfied," he said to the officers. But other cases weren't so simple. Ludwig invented illnesses to protect the healthy. He stepped behind the officers and made faces, encouraging his fake patients to moan and act sick. Ludwig risked his own life with this stunt.

A synagogue in Berlin is destroyed during Kristallnacht, 1938

After several hours, the Gestapo officers were convinced. Ludwig had saved the lives of sixty men. But four were taken away by the soldiers. Some doctors were taken, too. "You will stay here for the time being and will report every day to me," one of the officers barked at Ludwig. "Nothing irregular happens here in the hospital."

That afternoon Ludwig took another risk—he reported the incident to the Nazi Health Ministry. Surprisingly, his complaint was heard. After several weeks, his doctors were released from the concentration camps. Their fingers were

numb with frostbite. They had lost weight from starvation and illness. Some had been beaten. All had their hair shaved off. The doctors were now patients in their own hospital.

A few weeks later Ludwig faced another demand from the Nazi government. They wanted him to travel to Portugal to operate on a friend of the Portuguese prime minister. The mission was critical to Nazi Germany. They wanted to remain in good standing with Portugal, a country that controlled the mining of tungsten, a rare metal required for weapons production.

Like other Jews, Ludwig had had his passport seized by the Gestapo. Now it was quickly returned to him. But the Nazis' travel request was the last straw for Ludwig. This same government had taken his medical license, forbidden him from treating non-Jewish citizens, and wouldn't even call him doctor. Ludwig had seen too much unfair treatment of the Jewish people. Too much violence. Too much sadness.

A second world war loomed. It was time for Ludwig to make a difficult decision.

When he returned from Portugal, he was granted permission for a three-day trip to London, England. He had secretly been in contact with a British organization called the Society for the Protection of Science and Learning. They arranged the travel visas Ludwig would need to leave Germany for good. He sent a two-word telegram to his wife: "Start packing."

Chapter 7

YEARS OF CHANGE

The Guttmanns gathered their clothes, books, and a few of Ludwig's surgical tools. Customs officers, who had been notified that the Guttmanns were leaving Germany, arrived to supervise the packing of their bags. Money, jewelry, and other valuables could not be taken, as they were needed to pay costly moving taxes to the Nazis. The family was left with only forty marks for their travels (about sixteen dollars total). Ludwig stood in the open doorway, looking at his home for the last time. His wife sobbed. They were leaving the land where they grew up, where their children were born, where their family and friends remained in uncertain conditions.

On a wet, gray day in March 1939 the Guttmanns arrived in Oxford, England. They stayed in housing on the university campus as guests of the headmaster until they found a place of their own. With so little money, they settled on an apartment much smaller than their old home. Ludwig was relieved that his family was safe, but so much had changed. The weather in England was dreary. The family spoke little English. The children started new schools without their old friends.

Thankfully, Ludwig still had his medical career. But when he offered his services as a surgeon, he was given a position doing research instead. He would not have the opportunity to treat patients. It seemed his old boss and teacher, Dr. Foerster, was not as highly regarded in England as he was in Germany. Ludwig's experience did not hold the same importance here.

A few months later, when England entered the Second World War, Ludwig offered to work for the British Army. He was more than qualified to treat wounded soldiers. But again his request was denied. So Ludwig spent the next years conducting research on the human nervous system; specifically, how nerves functioned in people with injuries or illnesses affecting their spine.

Nervous System

The nervous system is like a communication center. It allows messages to be sent back and forth between the brain and the rest of the body. The nervous system is made of two parts: the *central nervous system* (CNS) and the *peripheral nervous system* (PNS). The central nervous system includes the brain and the spinal cord. The peripheral nervous system contains all the nerves, like long wires, that connect the brain and spine to every other part of the body. There are two types of nerves: *motor nerves* and *sensory nerves*. Motor nerves send signals from the brain to the body. They tell muscles how to move. Sensory nerves send signals from the body to the brain. They relay information about the outside world through sight, smell, sound, taste, and touch. Some of the nerves in the PNS work automatically, without us thinking about them. They make lungs breathe, hearts pump, feet sweat, and stomachs digest food. These nerves are called *autonomic*. Other nerves, called *somatic*, are under our control. They allow us to run, jump, or move our bodies any other way we please.

Ludwig designed a clever experiment using a special powder dye called quinizarin. The powder was light gray when dry and dark purple when wet. Here's how the experiment worked: A research subject lay on a hospital bed with clothing removed. The subject was coated with a dusting of

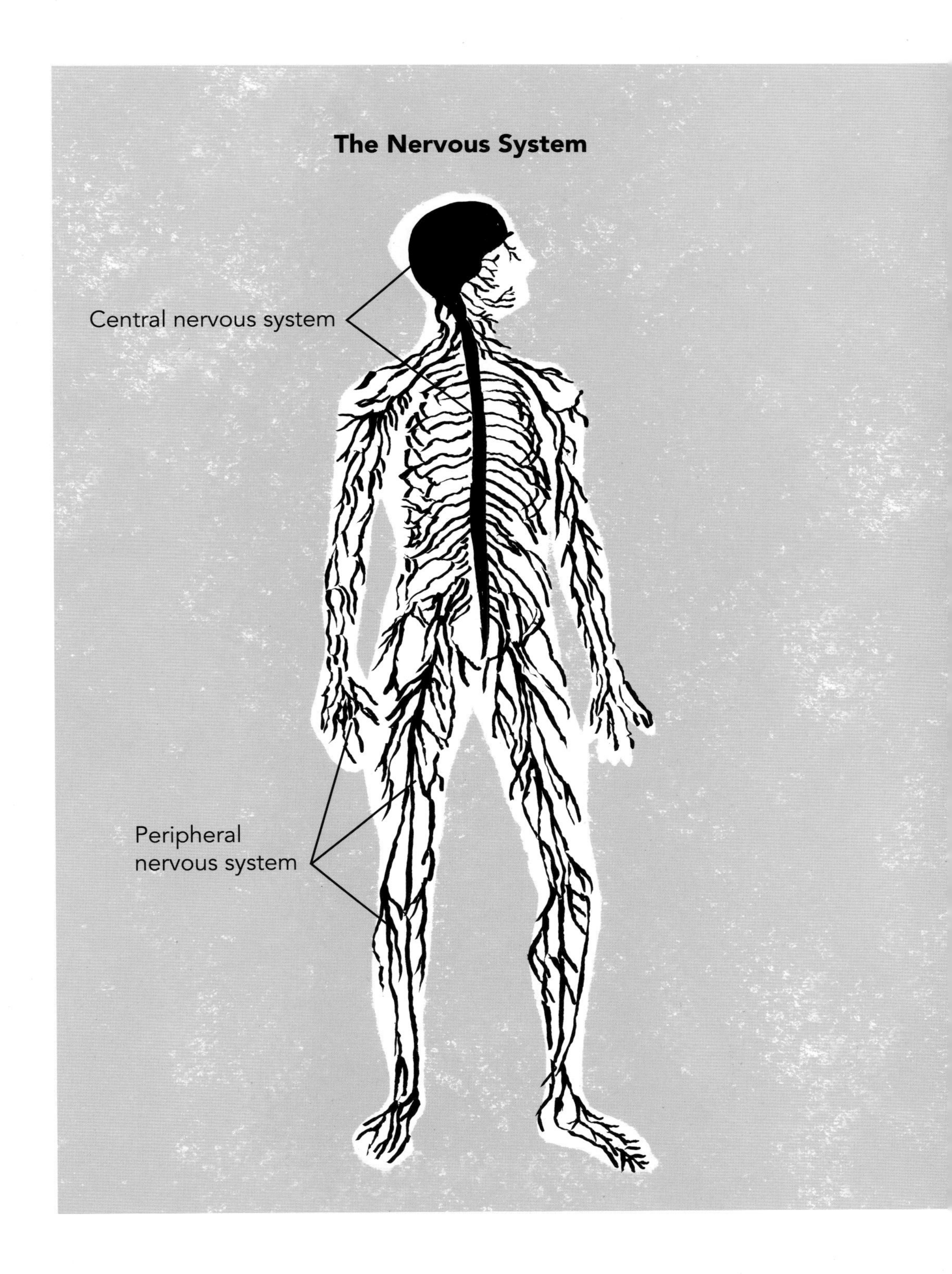
The Nervous System
Central nervous system
Peripheral
nervous system

the dye. Then the bed was wheeled into a large contraption called a sweat box.

Inside the box, hot air circulated. When the test subject began to sweat, the powder dye turned purple. Sweat glands are controlled by autonomic nerves under the skin. A person doesn't have to think about sweating—it happens automatically. In subjects with spinal damage, certain nerves no longer received the signal to sweat. So some of their powder dye remained gray. Ludwig now had a map of the peripheral nervous system and could see which nerves were damaged and which were still working.

Ludwig's findings were published in scientific journals. The papers were important, but after nearly five years,

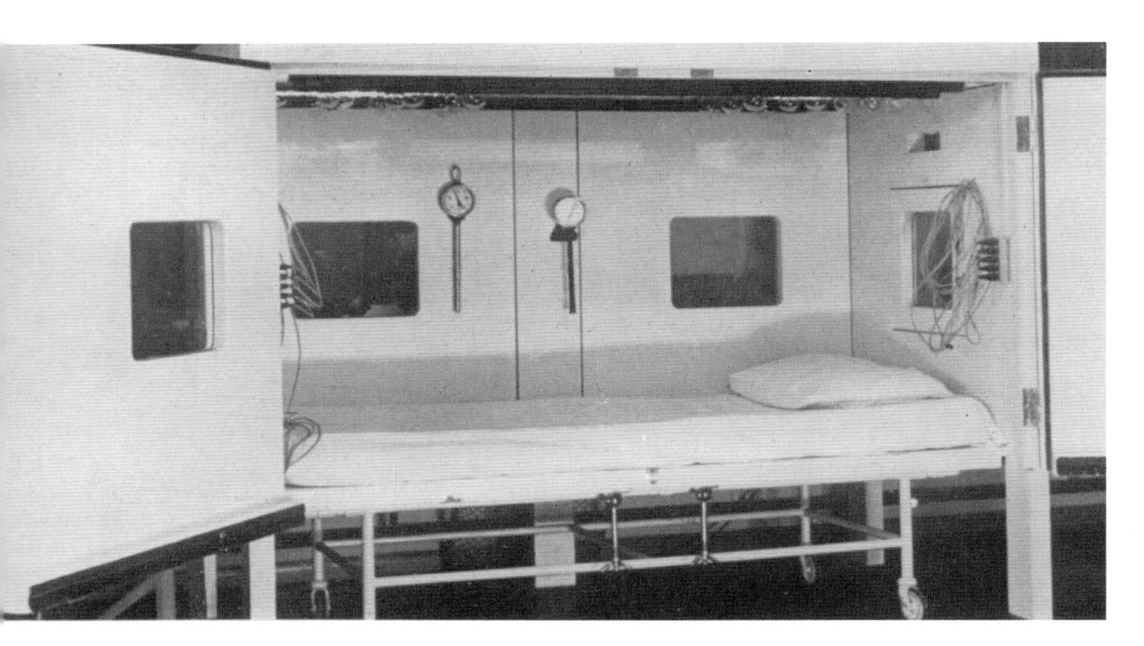

Ludwig's sweat box

Ludwig was tired of research. He missed treating patients at the hospital. Young doctors, who knew little of Ludwig's medical experience in Germany, didn't take him seriously. They teased him with the nickname "Sweaty Guttmann" because of his research with the heater box.

Finally, in September 1943, a London neurosurgeon and medical officer for the British Army took notice of Ludwig's research. Dr. George Riddoch asked Ludwig to take the lead of a new medical unit, opening at Stoke Mandeville Hospital, about forty miles northwest of London. After four years of World War II, hundreds of soldiers had suffered spinal injuries and needed treatment.

Ludwig was excited to work with patients again. But his coworkers at Oxford University thought the offer seemed like a dead-end job, hopeless and depressing. Even so, Ludwig was up to the challenge as long as he could treat patients his own way. He believed very few spinal injuries required surgery. This idea conflicted with other doctors' theories at the time. Ludwig's unique view was based on his research at Oxford and his experience back in Germany. He told Dr. Riddoch, "I must have a free hand to find out whether my philosophy can be put into practice." Dr. Riddoch agreed to the terms and left Ludwig with few instructions on how to manage his new unit. He said only, "You will have to start from scratch."

Chapter 8

LUDWIG'S INCURABLES

Like many hospitals during wartime, Stoke Mandeville was crowded with soldiers wounded in battle. German planes dropped bombs over British cities, so civilians had been injured as well. Rows of temporary huts were assembled outside the main hospital to accommodate the overflow. Ludwig converted one of these empty wooden buildings, Ward X, into his Spinal Injuries Center. The structure had room for twenty-six metal beds. He was assigned a staff of two nurses and eight orderlies. On March 1, 1944, three days after Ludwig arrived, he received his first patient.

Wood engraving shows American James Norris, in a restraining device, seated on a straw bed in Bethlem Royal Hospital, sometimes known as Bedlam, London, England, 1814.

Ludwig quickly learned that his staff was not prepared to care for the wounded soldier. Many of the young orderlies had never worked with patients. And the nurses did not want to fuss over a soldier who had little hope of surviving his injury. The nurses preferred not to work with Ludwig either. The German refugee was an outsider at the British hospital. Most employees felt the new unit was a waste of time and money. Their opinion about spinal injury patients was obvious: "The view generally held was the sooner they died the better for all concerned."

Ludwig did not want Ward X to be a last stop, a place where unwanted patients came to die. He developed a radical new plan. Instead of isolating patients, he would provide them with more care than ever before. Ludwig believed his methods would rescue people with paraplegia from "the human scrapheap" and return them to "a life worth living, as useful and respected

Treatment of People with Disabilities Throughout History

People with disabilities have experienced unfair and cruel treatment for centuries. In ancient times it was not uncommon for blind people, deaf people, people with cerebral palsy, epilepsy, mental health conditions, or physical disabilities to be burned, drowned, abandoned, or killed in other ways. As late as the early 1900s doctors labeled people with disabilities defective. Parents were encouraged to admit their loved ones into correctional institutions so they would not be a burden to their families. Overcrowded wards meant patients faced abuse or neglect. In 1939, Hitler ordered the killing of "the incurably ill," as he viewed these individuals "useless" and "unworthy of life." Between 1940 and 1945, about two hundred thousand people with disabilities were killed under Nazi leadership, in gas chambers, by poisonous injection, or by starvation. Perceptions began to change after World War II. With so many injured soldiers, laws were enacted to help with rehabilitation and reentry into the workforce. Sending people away to institutions became less common as doctors learned more about the correct types of treatment for different patients. Other laws were passed to improve the way children and adults with disabilities were treated in school and work settings. Today laws continue to expand to provide people with disabilities fair and equal treatment.

citizens in the community." No one thought it was possible —not even the patients. Soldiers who were once strong and active were shocked to learn that they could no longer walk, dress themselves, use the bathroom, or do any of the small things they used to take for granted. When patients found out there was no cure, many wanted to give up and die. Ludwig saw a future for these patients, even when they could not.

The first step in Ludwig's new treatment plan was to address full-body casts. They had to go! Although the casts helped to transport wounded soldiers from the battlefield, they also caused bedsores. Infected sores could spread deadly bacteria throughout the body. Under Ludwig's direction, when a new patient arrived in the unit the cast was cut off immediately. Now the patient rested on a bed of soft pillows. Ludwig carefully measured the sores along the spine and on the back of the shoulders, hips, and heels. He traced their shapes onto clear film. He sprinkled on a new antibiotic powder, called penicillin. Each day, he measured and traced. He taught his staff to measure and trace as well. They wondered if all the extra work was really necessary.

With no feeling in their lower body, the patients had trouble changing positions in bed. To keep new sores from forming, the staff was ordered to turn each patient. Front to back. Side to side. Every two hours, day and night. The heavy lifting was hard work for the nurses and orderlies. And the patients hated to be woken from sleep. Everyone complained. But Ludwig insisted! He visited the ward at all hours to be sure his staff was turning each and every patient.

Soon the wounds began to heal and shrink. The simple routine may have been tedious, but it was making a difference.

Ludwig had another issue to tackle. With the loss of feeling, spinal injury patients could not sense a full bladder. Infection spread to the kidneys when urine was held for too long. Most doctors performed a surgery, cutting through the abdomen and into the bladder to insert a tube, then attaching a small box to the belly to collect urine. The procedure was supposed to reduce the risk of infection, but often the incisions would not heal, making matters worse. Ludwig tried something different. He inserted a tube into the bladder from the urethra, the duct that allows urine to normally

drain from the body. Ludwig completed all of these catheterizations himself, using strict sterile procedures. Urine could now pass without the risk of infection from surgery.

Ludwig was careful to avoid any type of unnecessary surgery. When other doctors recommended operating on the spinal cord, Ludwig overruled them and called their actions "irresponsible meddling." He knew surgery could cause bleeding, bruising, and further damage to the spine. Based on his years of research, Ludwig believed most spinal damage was better left to heal on its own.

Few people won an argument with Ludwig. He demanded that his treatment plan be followed exactly. While his direct manner didn't always win friends, it got results. Within a year, Ludwig and his team had drastically improved the life expectancy of their patients. After World War I, about 80 percent of patients with a broken spine would die within one year. Now 80 percent of Stoke Mandeville patients with broken spines were surviving their first year and beyond.

Dr. Riddoch was so pleased with the progress that he directed all British soldiers with spinal injuries be sent straight to Stoke Mandeville. Beds filled rapidly, and three wards were added. Word spread through the hospital about the stubborn doctor with the German accent. But now nurses and orderlies wanted to work alongside Ludwig. He was changing minds about the fate of spinal injury patients.

Ludwig's dedication was inspiring. He seemed to live for the job. In fact, Ludwig rarely went home. He had a bed placed in his office and often slept at the hospital.

Chapter 9

THE RETURN OF HOPE

Now that major medical problems such as bedsores and bladder infections were under control, Ludwig felt it was time for another radical idea: spinal injury patients should not be kept in bed. They should be encouraged to move. This came as a shock to the patients. Most had been told they'd never walk again. Why bother getting out of bed?

Ludwig began slowly. First, he wanted his patients to sit up. When Reg Townsend, a World War II soldier who was paralyzed by flying shrapnel tried to sit, he quickly complained of dizziness and nausea. So did the other patients. But Ludwig insisted. With help from the staff, Reg and others practiced for a few minutes each day until they were all sitting comfortably.

Ludwig did not stop there. Wooden parallel bars were installed in the middle of the wards. He asked specialists called physical therapists to get his patients out of bed. The physical therapists didn't believe it was possible—it had never been tried before. But again Ludwig insisted. Reg was fitted with special leg braces. Before long, he was using his upper body strength to take a few steps. Everyone in the ward cheered! Who wanted to try next?

Learning to Sit

Many paralyzed patients feel dizzy when they first begin to sit, especially *tetraplegics,* patients who have damaged the highest part of their spine and have lost feeling in the torso and all four limbs. Blood pressure is difficult to regulate after their injuries. When patients are tilted upright, pressure decreases and not enough blood flows to the brain. This can result in nausea, dizziness, or even fainting. Repeating the process daily, a few minutes at a time, helps patients adjust to a sitting position.

Ludwig training physical therapists, 1949

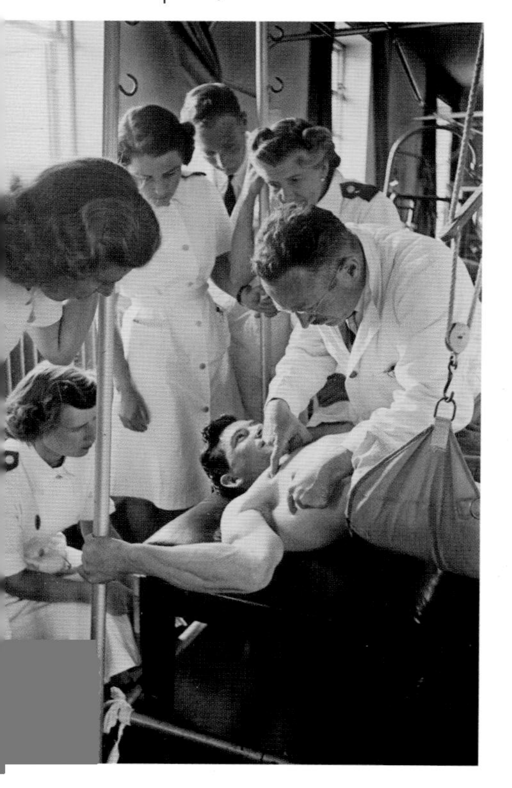

Although the brief walking sessions were a success, Ludwig was still not satisfied. He blew through the hospital hallways like a tornado, determined to find what he was looking for. Wheelchairs! With their stiff wooden seats and high backs, they looked more like dining room chairs on wheels. They were heavy and difficult to maneuver, but they would do. Soon Ludwig's patients were on the move.

But they had nowhere to go.

Nothing to do.

What now?

Ludwig had another idea. He asked his secretary, Joan Scruton, to grab a pen and paper. They surveyed each patient. Joan took notes.

What are your hopes?

What are your hobbies?

Do you want to play an instrument?

How about learning a new skill?

Until now, there was no use asking these kinds of questions. Most patients died soon after their injury with little hope of returning to their old life. Although they couldn't use their legs, Ludwig's patients were healthy and strong once again. He believed they should be mastering simple tasks,

like how to dress themselves and fix their own meals, or even learning job skills. He wanted movement to be "purposeful." It wasn't unusual to hear Ludwig encourage his patients with words such as "don't be lazy" or "help yourself." He hoped this occupational therapy would prepare them to leave the hospital, find work, and live a useful life.

At the rear of the hospital stood a repair shop filled with woodworking tools. A hospital employee, Bill Parker, agreed to help Ludwig turn the space into a vocational training area, a center for teaching the patients new skills. They learned woodworking, toy making, clock and watch repair, shoe repair, engraving, and typing. Some patients studied academics, eventually earning degrees in accounting or law. Others tried their hand at writing for *The Cord,* a magazine Ludwig started for people with spinal injuries. A few patients tried jobs in a nearby factory, successfully completing a full day's work. There were opportunities to play music in a band, sing in a choir, put on plays, and visit the local pub. Ludwig kept his patients so busy that one joked, "There's no bloody time to be ill in this bloody place."

The Spinal Injuries Center at Stoke Mandeville was one of a kind. The mood in the ward was cheerful. Ludwig had a special way with his patients—caring but firm. He pushed and persuaded them out of their beds and into the world. The patients began to show the same fighting spirit as Ludwig himself. They gave Ludwig a loving nickname: Poppa.

I would not recommend paraplegia to anybody as a career, but if it falls your way there is only one place to go, and there you will find the finest team in the world, led, as from the beginning, by one man.

—Reg Townsend, World War II soldier and patient of Dr. Ludwig Guttmann

Ludwig was pleased with the progress. But when family and friends arrived, their faces sank with sadness, their eyes darted to the floor. Instead of seeing the hard-learned skills, visitors saw only what the patients could no longer do. An injured army chaplain took note of this attitude and wrote in his journal, "The first duty of the paraplegic patient is to cheer up his visitors."

Ludwig wanted the pity to stop. There had to be a way to convince family, friends, and the general public that these men and women were more than their injuries. But how?

Chapter 10

A GAME CHANGER

One sunny lunchtime, just outside the wards, Ludwig spotted a group of his patients swiveling wildly in their wheelchairs. They slapped at the ground with some sort of sticks. What could they possibly be doing? Ludwig took a closer look.

The patients maneuvered their bulky wheelchairs with one hand while holding an upside-down walking cane in the other. When a small wooden puck slid within reach—WHACK!—it was sent flying with a slap of the stick. A player who shot the puck past the wheelchairs scored a goal.

The game looked a bit like polo, but instead of riding on horses, the players moved in wheelchairs. Or like hockey without the skates.

Ludwig couldn't take his eyes off the action. Until now, he had encouraged his patients to play simple games such as darts to help pass the time. Other exercises, such as catch with a weighted ball, helped patients build upper body strength. But this match on the lawn was something else entirely. Could his patients play *team* sports? Could they *compete* against one another?

Ludwig slipped into an empty wheelchair and joined the group. Some of the physical therapists tried, too. Having legs that worked was no help in this sport. Ludwig quickly learned that the patients in wheelchairs were better at passing and

Wheelchair polo on the lawn of Stoke Mandeville, circa 1945

scoring than the non-disabled staff. He was convinced that exercise could help "develop new tricks for making muscles move parts of the body formerly moved by other muscles." Playtime was over for Ludwig. But the game gave him an idea. He updated his treatment plan for all patients:

Wake, dress, eat, walk, work . . . play sports!

Before long, more teams faced off in rowdy wheelchair polo matches. Some days the patients played against the

More Than a Game

Playing sports does much more for your body than strengthen muscles. During exercise, the brain releases *endorphins.* These chemicals lift your mood and reduce feelings of stress. Scientists have found that learning a new sport or skill (in one experiment, participants were taught how to juggle) strengthens nerve connections in the *motor cortex,* the part of the brain that controls movement. In addition, researchers have found that aerobic exercise (running, swimming, biking, or any other activity that strengthens your heart and lungs) increases the number of cells in certain areas of your brain. One such area is the *hippocampus,* the part of the brain associated with memory and learning. Regular exercise can change how you think and feel by improving concentration, boosting confidence, and even helping you sleep better.

The Human Brain

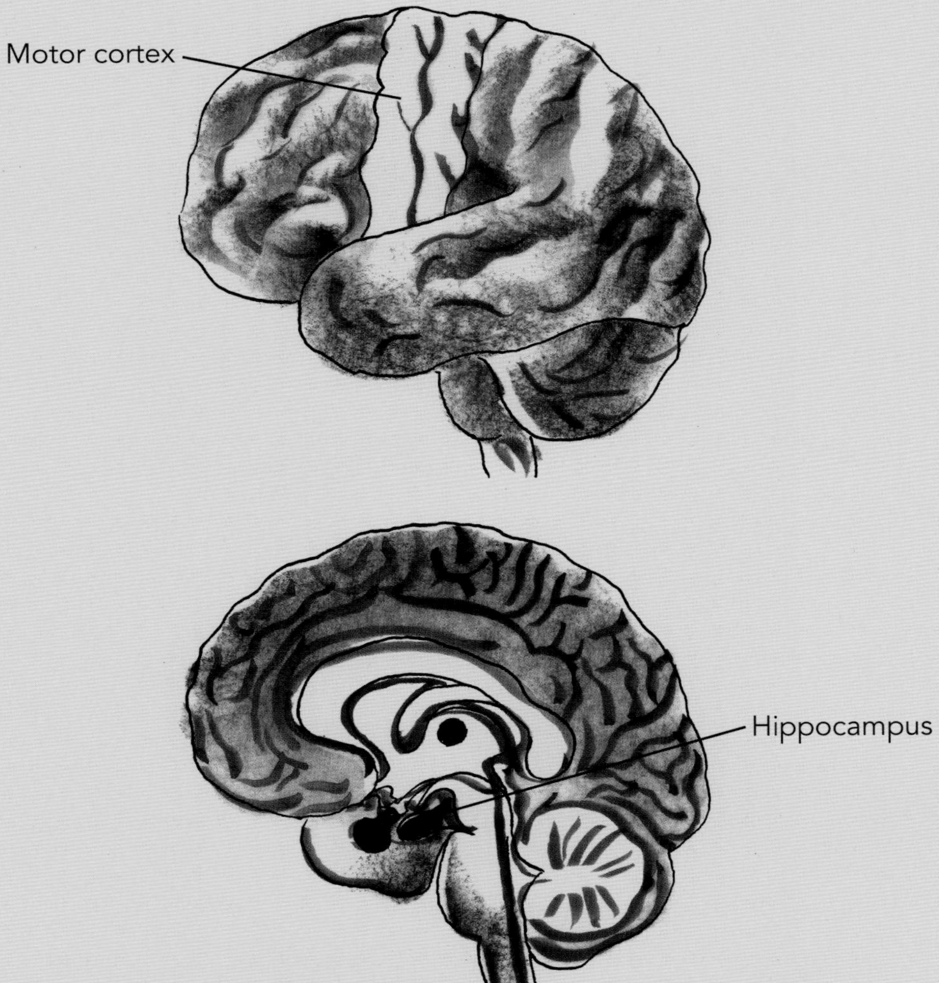

Motor cortex

Hippocampus

hospital staff. Some days they played against one another. Most of Ludwig's patients were young soldiers. They had enjoyed playing or watching sports before their injury. Even the patients who were new to sports were eager to try. Hearts and muscles grew stronger. Friendships grew, too. The team spirit was contagious!

But Ludwig's bosses, the doctors who ran the hospital, did not care for the ruckus on the lawn. The crashing wheelchairs, the injured men on display for all to see—they worried what hospital visitors would think. They wanted the games to stop immediately. In addition, the clashing sticks and bashing wheelchairs left players with cuts and bruises. Ludwig had no choice. He put an end to wheelchair polo.

But ultimately, Ludwig went against his bosses' orders. He encouraged patients to continue with sports out on the lawn. Ludwig had a safer idea for their next match—wheelchair netball, which later became known as wheelchair basketball.

Basketball quickly became a ward favorite. But the competition didn't stop there. One afternoon Ludwig entered the ward clutching a bow, arrows, and a wild new idea: "We [are] going to teach the patients archery!" He invited a champion archer to Stoke Mandeville to give lessons. Archery was perfect for strengthening arms, shoulders, and the abdominal and back muscles that help a paralyzed person sit upright and balanced. After a good deal of practice, Ludwig's patients hit the center target with ease. Some became so skilled, they played against non-disabled competitors without any changes to the rules of the sport. They traveled around the city in a special bus modified to fit wheelchairs. By participating in archery tournaments, Ludwig's patients began to show the community what they could do: build new relationships, compete with confidence, and oftentimes, win!

Game On!

Ludwig encouraged his patients to try different games and sports to pass the time and help strengthen their muscles while they recovered. Here are a few they played:

badminton

bowls—a game in which players roll a ball (called a bowl) up a green trying to finish closest to a smaller white ball (called a jack)

javelin

netball—a team sport in which each team tries to score goals by passing a ball down the court and shooting it through a goal ring

skittles—a game similar to bowling in which a heavy ball is rolled to knock over nine pins

snooker—a game similar to billiards in which a cue stick and cue ball are used to knock remaining balls into side and corner pockets

table tennis

Chapter 11

THE STOKE MANDEVILLE GAMES

On July 29, 1948, Ludwig hosted an archery competition on the Stoke Mandeville lawn. Sixteen ex-service members, fourteen men and two women, from two hospitals participated in front of a few dozen spectators.

The first competitor aligned her wheelchair with a target across the grass. She placed an arrow to her bow and slowly pulled back the string—ready, aim, release! The arrow sliced through the air, barely missing the center target. Could the next person do better?

The competition lasted all afternoon. At the end of the day Ludwig presented a trophy to the Star and Garter Home, the hospital with the highest score. Although the demonstration was small, Ludwig proved that sports are for everyone. Only thirty-five miles from Stoke Mandeville, the opening ceremony of the Olympic Games was under way in London. Was it a coincidence that Ludwig scheduled his archery competition the very same day?

Ludwig and his coworkers continued to host the Stoke Mandeville Games every July. At first people laughed at the idea. They told Ludwig that wheelchair sports were ridiculous. They said no one would watch. But that didn't stop him. By 1959, the annual event had grown from the original 16 archers to more than 350 athletes. They came from twenty countries to compete in eleven different sports. The number of spectators grew as well.

Growth of the Stoke Mandeville Games Over the First Five Years

Date	Competitors	Countries	Sports
July 29, 1948	16	Great Britain (2 hospitals)	archery
July 29, 1949	60	Great Britain (6 hospitals)	archery netball
July 27, 1950	61	Great Britain (10 hospitals)	archery netball javelin
July 28, 1951	126	Great Britain (11 hospitals)	archery netball javelin snooker
July 26, 1952*	130	Great Britain Netherlands	archery netball javelin snooker table tennis

**In 1952 the Stoke Mandeville Games began tracking the number of countries in attendance, rather than the number of hospitals participating.*

A British and Dutch team face off in netball, Stoke Mandeville Games, 1953

Ludwig's budget was still small, so everyone had to pitch in. Events were run by nurses and physical therapists. Ludwig's children helped remove arrows from archery targets. His wife served snacks at a big party after the last event.

The Stoke Mandeville Games were a celebration. Sports brought passion and fun back into patients' lives. Dick Thompson was one such athlete. A star javelin thrower in high school, he stopped competing at seventeen after a fall from a climbing accident paralyzed him from the chest down. "Those Games changed the whole course of my life.

[Ludwig] gave me an interest in something I never thought I would ever do again." In 1950, Dick won the Stoke Mandeville javelin event. Even better, Ludwig organized a demonstration in which Dick competed against a non-disabled athlete—the current British javelin champion! To keep things fair, an empty wheelchair was rolled onto the lawn for the match-up. With both athletes throwing from a seated position, Dick's javelin swiftly sailed past his com-

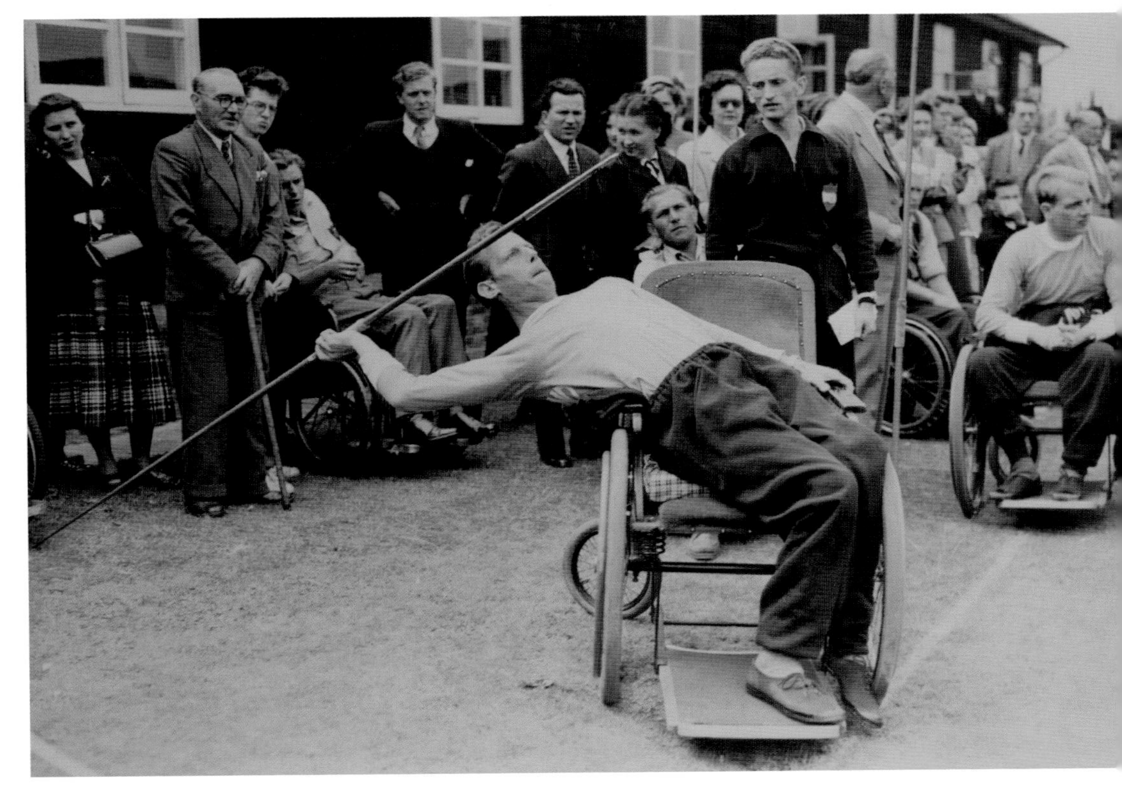

Javelin throw from a Dutch athlete at the Stoke Mandeville Games, 1954

petitor's javelin. The crowd burst into applause. When Dick looked at Ludwig, he saw "a great beam all over his face."

Ludwig was sure when the public witnessed these men and women successfully competing in sporting events, it would be easier to accept them as regular people who could work, learn, and play, just like anyone else. Friends and family left the Stoke Mandeville Games with something as well—an improved attitude. They saw that lives were not ruined by spinal injury.

The Games became as important to Ludwig as his medical tasks inside the hospital. He and his patients wrote about

First Parade of Nations at the close of the Stoke Mandeville Games, 1954

the annual competition in *The Cord.* The magazine was now popular with paraplegics and was mailed to hospitals near and far. During his travels to medical conferences, Ludwig challenged other cities to send a team of athletes to the next year's event. He also encouraged his former patients to spread the word about the Stoke Mandeville Games.

Much had changed since the first archery demonstration on the lawn. In 1952 the Games became international when a small group of Dutch athletes traveled from a hospital in the Netherlands to compete. In 1953, with money raised by Ludwig, a heated indoor swimming pool was built near the

Ludwig welcomes athletes, 1954

hospital. Swimming events were soon added to the Games. In 1957 competitors arrived from six continents to give the Games a try. Stars were added to the flag each year as more countries took part. In 1958 so many British athletes wanted to participate, a smaller set of qualifying games was held beforehand to select a team.

Even though the Stoke Mandeville Games had grown, Ludwig was not satisfied. His greatest dream was for the Games to become as popular and widely recognized as the most famous sporting event in the world—the Olympics. Perhaps Ludwig was motivated in small part by the Olympic Creed, which fit hand in hand with his own beliefs: *The most important thing in the Olympic Games is not to win but to take part, just as the most important thing in life is not the triumph but the struggle. The essential thing is not to have conquered but to have fought well.*

Chapter 12

WHEELS IN MOTION

Family and friends weren't the only people watching the Stoke Mandeville Games. In 1956 a surgeon and member of the International Olympic Committee, Sir Arthur Porritt, attended the events. He cheered for wheelchair basketball. Wheelchair fencing kept him on the edge of his seat. Porritt was impressed by the athletes' abilities. And he was impressed by something else—their friendship, unity, and good sportsmanship. He told a local newspaper, "The spirit of these Games goes beyond the Olympic Games spirit. You

compete not only with skill and endurance but with courage and bravery too." Porritt recommended the Stoke Mandeville Games for a prestigious award. Six months later, Ludwig accepted the Fearnley Cup for achievement in supporting the ideals of the Olympic Games.

The special award helped pave the way to a huge milestone for disability sports—the moment Ludwig had been waiting for. In 1960 the Stoke Mandeville Games were invited abroad, to Rome, Italy, the city hosting the Summer Olympics. Nearly four hundred

The Italian team entering last, as hosts. Rome, 1960

wheelchair athletes from twenty-one countries participated. On the evening of September 18 a crowd gathered around the track for the opening ceremony. A police band set the mood with lively music. Next came the Parade of Nations. The British team led the way as founders of the Stoke Mandeville Games. The remaining teams wheeled in alphabetically by country with Italy last, as hosts.

Flags flapped in the wind while speeches welcomed. A full week of sporting competition followed. Maria Scutti of Italy won the most medals—ten golds and fifteen medals in total. Although she had lost the use of her legs after a car accident, she participated in fencing, swimming, table

Margaret Maughan wins the first gold medal for the British team at the first Paralympic Games. She was sent to Stoke Mandeville for treatment after a car accident severed her spine. Rome, 1960

tennis, shot put, and javelin. As a country, Italy brought home the most medals (eighty) with Great Britain following (fifty-five).

At the conclusion of the Games, Pope John XXIII gave a speech to the athletes: "You are the living demon-

Great Britain's first gold medal at the first Paralympic Games, 1960

stration of the marvels of the virtue of energy . . . you have shown what an energetic soul can achieve, in spite of apparently insurmountable obstacles imposed by the body."

Ludwig's dream had become a reality. The Stoke Mandeville Games had been played alongside the Olympics. The Greek word *para-* means "alongside" or "in parallel." Later renamed, the 1960 event in Rome was recorded as the first official Paralympic Games.

Four years later, following the Olympics schedule, wheelchair athletes competed in Tokyo, Japan, after the Summer Olympics. More than one hundred thousand spectators filled stadium seats. Ludwig remarked, "The Tokyo Games were outstanding in demonstrating the effect of sport of the disabled on society as a whole." In fact, the Games began to change the culture in Japan, a place where people with disabilities were made to feel ashamed of their condition and were often hidden away in remote facilities. Not only

TOKYO 1964
SMG

British team traveling to the
Tokyo Paralympics, 1964

Poster from 1964 Paralympic Games

did citizens see men and women in wheelchairs on the playing fields, they saw them in town after the events, shopping, dining, and laughing with family and friends.

The Paralympic Games continued to take place every four years, following the Summer Olympics. More athletes participated, breaking more records. In 1976, the first Winter Paralympics were held in Örnsköldsvik, Sweden. The same year, athletes with disabilities other than spinal injuries, such as those who were amputees, blind, or visually impaired, began to compete.

Ludwig held fast to his belief that "sport is of even greater significance for the well-being of the severely disabled than the able-bodied." He saw how competition could help a

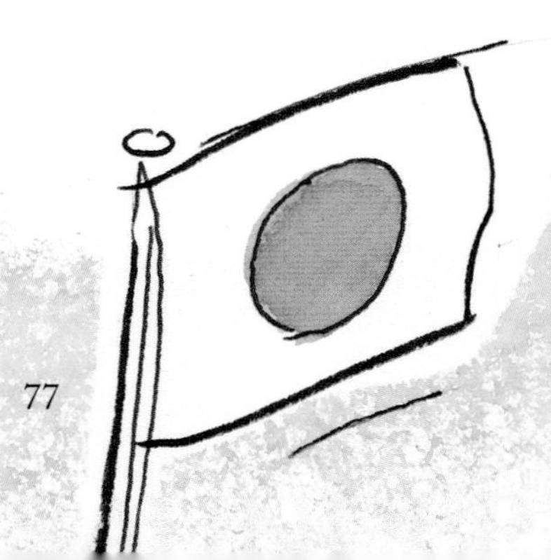

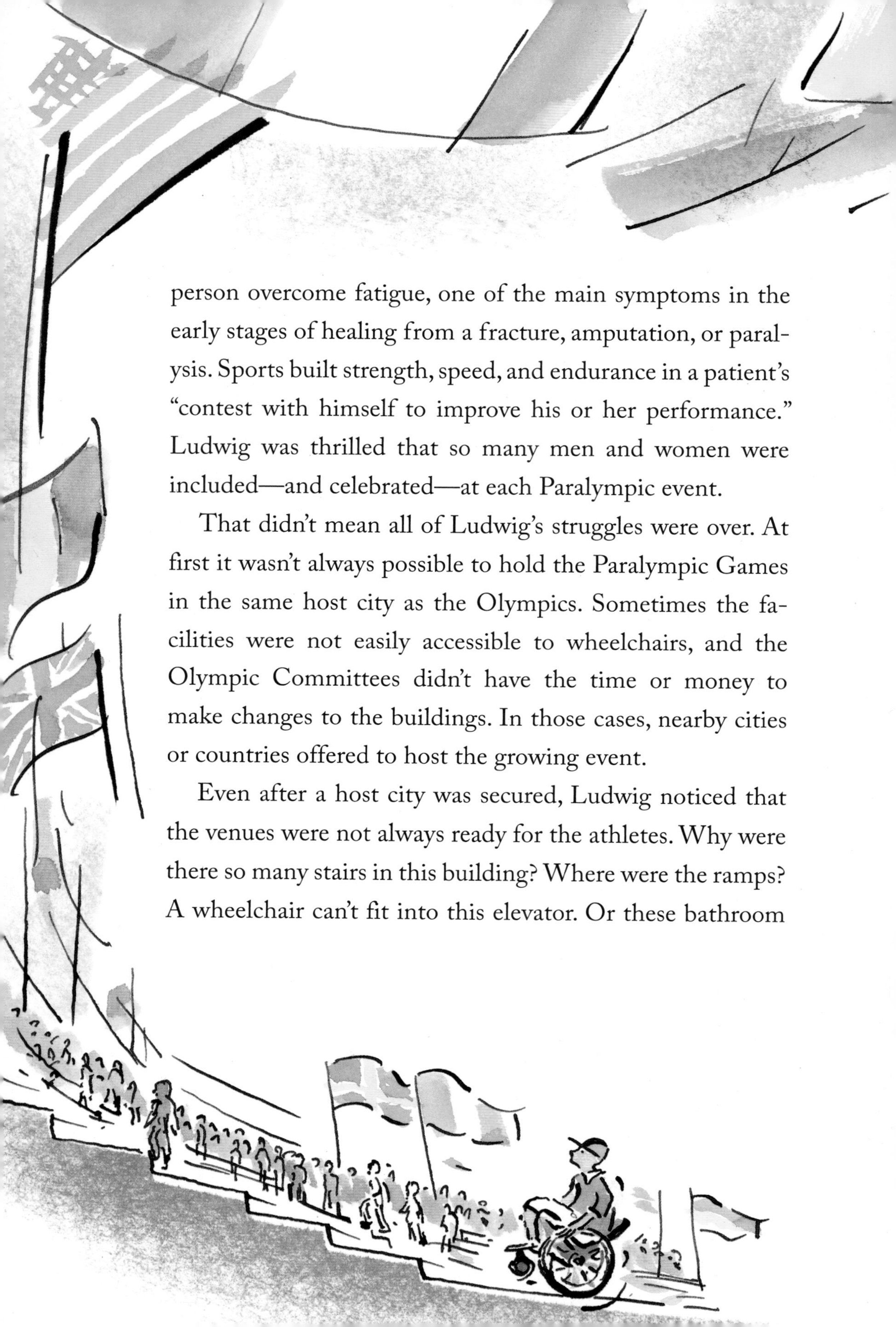

person overcome fatigue, one of the main symptoms in the early stages of healing from a fracture, amputation, or paralysis. Sports built strength, speed, and endurance in a patient's "contest with himself to improve his or her performance." Ludwig was thrilled that so many men and women were included—and celebrated—at each Paralympic event.

That didn't mean all of Ludwig's struggles were over. At first it wasn't always possible to hold the Paralympic Games in the same host city as the Olympics. Sometimes the facilities were not easily accessible to wheelchairs, and the Olympic Committees didn't have the time or money to make changes to the buildings. In those cases, nearby cities or countries offered to host the growing event.

Even after a host city was secured, Ludwig noticed that the venues were not always ready for the athletes. Why were there so many stairs in this building? Where were the ramps? A wheelchair can't fit into this elevator. Or these bathroom

Ludwig awarding medals at the Paralympic Games in Israel, 1968

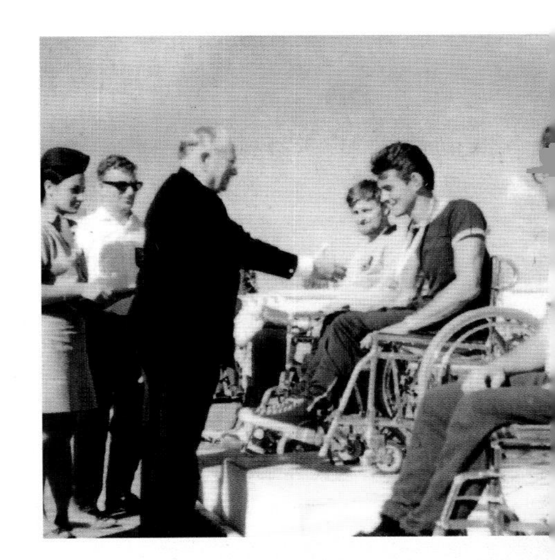

stalls! Air travel was difficult in the early years, as the athletes had to be lifted onto planes via forklift.

The lack of accessibility angered Ludwig. He constantly spoke up for the athletes' basic needs. Eventually, many cities enacted new laws to better allow people with disabilities to be part of society. From 1988 onward, the Paralympic Games would be held in the same host cities as the Summer and Winter Olympics.

Chapter 13

ONE GOOD THING

Ludwig's methods for success spread, although it would take time. In 1949, five years after the Spinal Injuries Center opened at Stoke Mandeville, a report on spinal units for the Ministry of Health stated, "Stoke Mandeville [is] the only satisfactory unit in the United Kingdom with an embarrassing number of applications for admission as a result of its high reputation." For the next twenty years Ludwig continued to share his innovative techniques. Doctors, students, and physical therapists came from around the world to learn. Some visits would be brief. Other visitors would stay more than a year before taking the methods home to their own hospitals. Ludwig traveled as well. He visited more than thirty countries in his career, helping other hospitals set up spinal units like the one at Stoke Mandeville. New centers in Germany, India, Spain, and Israel were all named after Ludwig. In 1963, Ludwig began a medical journal called *Paraplegia*, "to provide an international forum for an easy interchange of ideas for all those responsible for the welfare of our paralysed fellow men." The monthly journal is still published today under the name *Spinal Cord*.

Ludwig earned many honors and awards. He was knighted by Queen Elizabeth. He was made a Fellow by the Royal Society in London. He was invited to America to give lectures as a visiting professor. He even had a street in the Netherlands named after him. Ludwig wrote two books filled with everything he knew about spinal injuries. Doctors still read them today.

In 1967, at the age of sixty-seven, Ludwig retired from his position at the hospital. Before his retirement, he published a research paper about the first three thousand spinal injury patients admitted to Stoke Mandeville. Only 11 percent of Ludwig's patients died from their injury compared with 80 percent of patients who died from a broken spine after

Ludwig with members of the British team, 1960

World War I. The study also reported that over 85 percent of patients were employed in full- or part-time jobs such as teaching, working in shops and factories, or other professions.

Spinal units existed in Britain and America before Stoke Mandeville. Yet they all failed, even though many of their doctors knew the correct treatment for bedsores and bladder infections. Why was Ludwig successful when others were not?

Ludwig arrived at Stoke Mandeville skilled in neurology from his work in Germany and his years of research at Oxford. He was the only doctor who put all the treatment ideas together into one plan. And once the plan was set, Ludwig demanded that it be followed exactly. It's possible that Ludwig's success had less to do with his experience and more to do with his high standards, his drive, and his commanding personality.

Ludwig continued to travel, give lectures, and train other doctors until the end of his life. He died of heart failure on March 18, 1980, at the age of eighty, in Aylesbury, England. When Ludwig was asked about his biggest success, he could have pointed to the impressive statistics from his first three thousand patients. But for Ludwig, success was something closer to his heart: "If I ever did one good thing in my medical career, it was to introduce sport into the rehabilitation of disabled people."

Ludwig is remembered as a pioneer in the field of spinal cord injuries as well as the founding father of the Paralympic Games. Today the Paralympics are the third-largest sporting event in the world. In 2016 more than four thousand athletes competed in Rio de Janeiro, Brazil. The Games broke viewership records with a global television audience of more than 4.1 billion people.

Crowds cheering at 2016 Rio Paralympics

Chapter 14

GOING FOR GOLD

Trischa Zorn competes in the backstroke, 2004

Nearly two hundred countries have sent athletes to the Paralympics since 1960. Tens of thousands of athletes have competed. Here are a few of the men and women whose lives have been impacted by Ludwig and his founding of the Paralympic Games.

MOST DECORATED

Like many ten-year-olds living in sunny Southern California, Trischa Zorn loved to swim. But unlike most children, she was born with a visual impairment. Even though she could see faint, fuzzy shapes, she was declared legally blind. That didn't keep her from training alongside sighted swimmers. At the age of sixteen she participated in her first Paralympic Games in Arnhem, Netherlands, winning five gold medals. Over the next twenty-four years, Trischa participated in swimming events in six more Games. In Seoul, Korea, she won twelve gold medals, breaking Maria Scutti's record for most gold medals won in a single Paralympic Games, set in Rome in 1960. With 55 medals, Trischa is the most decorated Paralympic athlete of all time. She says, "I see people . . . with injuries and it really inspires me to make them appreciate what they have and to make them understand that whatever you set your mind to, you can do."

ROAD WARRIOR

At the age of fifteen, Franz Nietlispach fell from a cherry tree, permanently damaging his spine. But that didn't keep him from becoming one of Switzerland's most accomplished athletes. Franz competed in nine Paralympic Games from 1976 to 2008, collecting fourteen gold medals. He competed in forty-six wheelchair racing events, from short distances to team relays to the marathon (26.2 miles). "As I see it," Franz says, "sport is a perfect platform to reintegrate disabled athletes into society. Successful wheelchair athletes are role models." When an injury caused him to switch sports to hand cycling, he discovered a new passion—designing lightweight cycles for Paralympic athletes. In 2006 he founded the company Carbonbike, a leader in the industry today.

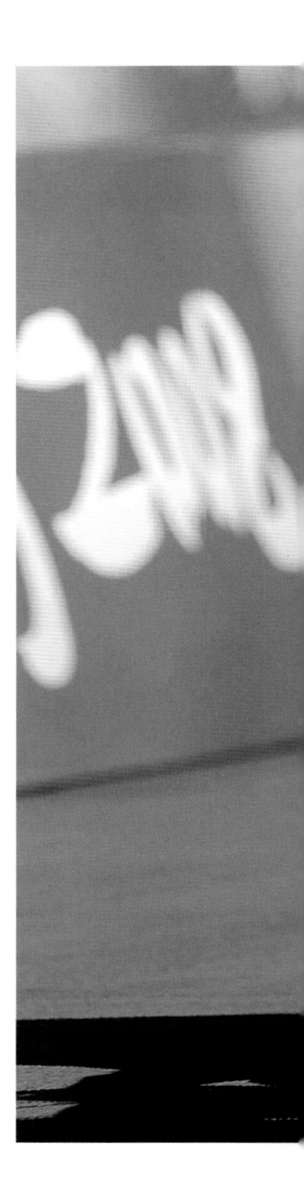

Franz Nietlispach races
on a Carbonbike, 2008

Declan Farmer battles with a
Canadian player for the puck, 2018

CHAMPION ON ICE

Declan Farmer was born with a condition that affected the bones in his lower legs, and he required a double amputation. An avid sports fan, he began playing sled hockey when he was eight years old. He recalls: "It was the fastest I'd ever moved before. I did soccer as a kid and that was really tough with two prosthetic legs, but with sled hockey, I just felt really free out there." In 2014, at the age of sixteen, he made his Paralympics debut in Sochi, Russia, winning a gold for Team USA and tying for the team lead in goals. In 2018, in Pyeongchang, South Korea, Declan took the team into overtime and scored the game-winning shot, sending the United States to the podium for gold once again.

BREAKING BARRIERS

Born with spina bifida, a condition that affected her spine and left her with no feeling in her legs, Tatyana McFadden lived the first six years of her life in a Russian orphanage. She had little food, few toys, and no access to a wheelchair. To keep up with the other children, Tatyana learned to walk with her hands. In 1994 she was adopted by an American family and brought to the United States. She was introduced to sports as a way to strengthen her body and meet new friends. Tatyana tried wheelchair basketball, swimming, ice hockey, and scuba diving before she fell in love with wheelchair racing. Only fifteen—the youngest competitor on Team USA—when she won her first two medals, Tatyana has been called one of the greatest wheelchair racers in the world. She helped to pass a federal law allowing students with disabilities the opportunity to be involved with sports in school. Tatyana keeps her personal motto simple: "You have the power to be anything you want to be."

Tatyana McFadden, shown competing in Rio de Janeiro, 2016, has participated in five Paralympic Games, winning a total of seventeen medals

Brian Bell in action, 2016

A LEADING SCORER

At age ten, Brian Bell lost his right leg in a train accident. After his treatment and recovery, Brian wanted to get back to playing his favorite sports: football and basketball. But football was difficult with a prosthetic leg. Brian couldn't keep up with other kids and was not as competitive as he wanted to be. Once he tried wheelchair basketball, he never looked back. When his wheelchair basketball team arrived in Rio de Janeiro in 2016, first-time Paralympian Brian was hopeful. "This is by far the best team I've been on athletically," he said. The US team went undefeated in Rio, beating Spain 68–52 in the gold medal match. Brian was one of the leading scorers, with 15 total points. "I want to show others that you can still go on to do great things even if you have a disability," said Brian. "It can make you stronger."

YEAR-ROUND ATHLETE

Muffy Davis could ski faster than any other girl or boy on the mountain in her hometown of Sun Valley, Idaho. At fourteen, she was named a US Junior Champion and was

Muffy shows her gold medals in cycling, 2012

Muffy Davis races down the super-G course, earning a silver medal, 2002

placed on a special team to prepare her to become an Olympic athlete. But early one morning when she was training, Muffy lost control and flew off the course at nearly fifty miles per hour. She crashed through the safety fence and smashed into a tree with her back. Muffy was paralyzed from the chest down. Several years later she learned about a ski camp for people with disabilities. She had lost strength in her torso and couldn't balance on the monoski, a small sled atop a single ski. But with time and practice, she began completing runs with fewer and fewer falls. In 1998, she headed to her first Paralympic Games in Nagano, Japan, where she earned a bronze medal in women's slalom. Four years later she won three silver medals in Salt Lake City, Utah. As a fun way to exercise in the summer months, Muffy began hand cycling. She qualified for the 2012 Summer Paralympics in London, where she won three gold medals. Describing competing in the Paralympics, she says, "I feel the same rush of adrenaline as any non-disabled athlete. The same rush I felt as a kid."

TIMELINE OF EVENTS

World events listed in blue.

1899 Ludwig Guttmann is born on July 3 in the German township of Tost, Upper Silesia, to Bernhard and Dorothea Guttmann.

1914 World War I begins.

1917 Ludwig graduates high school early. He volunteers at a local hospital as an orderly while he waits for military call-up.

At eighteen, Ludwig is denied entry into the German Army due to an ongoing infection in his neck.

1918 Ludwig begins medical school at the University of Breslau.

1919 World War I ends on June 28 with the signing of the Treaty of Versailles.

1923 Ludwig passes his final medical exams and begins training as a neurologist under Dr. Otfrid Foerster.

1927 Ludwig marries Else Samuel.

1928 Ludwig and Else move to Hamburg; Ludwig heads the neurology unit in a large university hospital.

1929 Ludwig and Else return to Breslau, upon urging from Dr. Foerster. Ludwig begins work as Foerster's neurology associate.

1929 Son, Dennis, is born.

1933 Daughter, Eva, is born.

January 30: The Nazi Party comes into power in Germany.

March 31: The Law for Restoration of the Professional Civil Service excludes Jews from holding government jobs.

April 1: Ludwig is fired from his position as head assistant under Dr. Foerster.

April 1: Nazi leadership organizes a boycott against Jewish shop owners and professionals. German citizens are encouraged to purchase goods and services elsewhere.

May 10: Books written by Jewish authors are publicly burned throughout Germany.

July 10: Ludwig begins a new job as head of neurology in an all-Jewish hospital in Breslau.

1934 After abolishing the office of president, Hitler becomes supreme leader of Germany. There are no constitutional limits to his power.

1936 The Summer Olympics are held in Berlin. Anti-Jewish activities stop temporarily in order for Germany to appear a respectable member of the international community.

1937 Ludwig is promoted to medical director of the Breslau Jewish Hospital.

1938 November 9–10: Kristallnacht, the Night of Broken Glass. Violent acts against Jewish citizens spread throughout Germany.

1939 March 14: Ludwig and his family flee Germany for Oxford, England.

April: Ludwig begins work as a research fellow in neurology at the Radcliffe Infirmary in Oxford, England.

September 1: World War II begins.

October: Hitler authorizes a euthanasia program to systematically kill disabled Germans whom the Nazis deem "unworthy of life."

1944 March 1: Ludwig opens the Spinal Injuries Center at Stoke Mandeville Hospital in Aylesbury, England, primarily to serve soldiers wounded in battle during World War II.

1945 September 2: World War II is officially over.

1948 July 29: The first Stoke Mandeville Games are held on the front lawn of the hospital. Sixteen ex-military members from two hospitals compete in one event—archery.

1952 In their fifth year, the Stoke Mandeville Games are considered an international event when a Dutch team of paraplegic war veterans compete in archery.

1955 The United States sends its first team to compete in the Stoke Mandeville Games.

1957 The Stoke Mandeville Games are awarded the Fearnley Cup for outstanding achievement in the service of the Olympic Movement.

1960 The Stoke Mandeville Games are played in Rome, Italy, to coincide with the Olympic Games. Later renamed, the 1960 event is recorded as the first official Paralympic Games.

1966 Ludwig is knighted by Queen Elizabeth for his services to people with disabilities. His title becomes Sir Ludwig Guttmann.

1967 At sixty-seven years of age, Ludwig retires as director of what is now recognized as the National Spinal Injuries Center at Stoke Mandeville Hospital.

1968 Ludwig raises funds to build the first sports stadium for people with disabilities on the grounds near Stoke Mandeville Hospital.

1976 Ludwig is elected Fellow of the Royal Society for his contributions to neuroscience.

The first Winter Paralympics take place in Örnsköldsvik, Sweden. Athletes with other disabilities (blind, visually impaired, amputees) begin to compete.

1980 Sir Ludwig Guttmann dies on March 18, 1980, at the age of eighty, in Aylesbury, England. The sports stadium he helped establish is renamed the Ludwig Guttmann Sports Center for the Disabled.

1988 From this year to the present, the Paralympic Games are held in the same host cities as the Summer and Winter Olympic Games.

2016 More than 4,000 athletes from 159 countries compete in the Paralympic Games in Rio de Janeiro, Brazil. The Games break viewership records, reaching a global television audience of more than 4.1 billion people.

NOTES

1. AN AILMENT NOT TO BE TREATED

1 *"I had the immediate sensation":* Goodman, *Spirit of Stoke Mandeville,* p. 130.

3 *"an ailment not to be treated":* Hughes, "Historical Review of Paraplegia."

6 *"incurables":* Goodman, *Spirit of Stoke Mandeville,* p. 98.

2. HEADSTRONG

8 *"a damned Jew":* Goodman, *Spirit of Stoke Mandeville,* p. 22.

3. THE MINER

12 *"I can't look at blood":* Goodman, *Spirit of Stoke Mandeville,* p. 28.

13 *"Dead in six weeks at the latest":* Ibid., p. 29.

15 *"We have enough cripples here!":* Ibid., p. 31.

15 *"War disabled":* Ibid.

4. A RETURN TO MEDICINE

17 *"scars of honor":* Goodman, *Spirit of Stoke Mandeville,* p. 40.

5. GROWING TENSION

24 *"master race":* US Holocaust Memorial Museum, "Learn About the Holocaust."

6. NIGHT OF BROKEN GLASS

30 *"How can you explain this?":* "Guttmann, Oral History," audio reel 2.

30 *"I take it you are satisfied":* Goodman, *Spirit of Stoke Mandeville,* p. 76.

31 *"Nothing irregular happens here in the hospital":* Ibid.

33 *"Start packing":* Imperial War Museums, "Guttmann, Oral History," audio reel 2.

7. YEARS OF CHANGE

39 *"Sweaty Guttmann":* Whitteridge, "Ludwig Guttmann," p. 233.

40 *"I must have a free hand":* Imperial War Museums, "Guttmann, Oral History," audio reel 3.

40 *"You will have to start from scratch":* Silver, "Treatment of Spinal Injuries," p. 92.

8. LUDWIG'S INCURABLES

42 *"The view generally held was":* Goodman, *Spirit of Stoke Mandeville*, p. 97.

42 *"the human scrapheap":* Goodman, *Spirit of Stoke Mandeville*, p. 101.

43 *"the incurably ill":* US Holocaust Memorial Museum, "Learn About the Holocaust."

46 *"irresponsible meddling"*: Ibid., p.107.

9. THE RETURN OF HOPE

51 *"purposeful":* Goodman, *Spirit of Stoke Mandeville*, p. 113.

51 *"help yourself":* Ibid.

52 *"There's no bloody time to be ill":* Ibid., p. 129.

53 *"I would not recommend paraplegia":* Ibid., p. 133.

53 *"The first duty of the paraplegic patient":* Whitteridge, "Ludwig Guttmann," p. 237.

10. A GAME CHANGER

56 *"develop new tricks":* Goodman, *Spirit of Stoke Mandeville*, p. 144.

59 *"We [are] going to teach the patients":* Ibid., p. 143.

11. THE STOKE MANDEVILLE GAMES

64 *"Those Games changed the whole course":* Goodman, *Spirit of Stoke Mandeville,* p. 154.

66 *"a great beam all over his face":* Ibid., p. 155.

12. WHEELS IN MOTION

69 *"The spirit of these Games":* Brittain, *Stoke Mandeville to Stratford*, p. 29.

72 *"You are the living demonstration":* Ibid., p. 58.

73 *"The Tokyo Games were outstanding":* Goodman, *Spirit of Stoke Mandeville,* p. 159.

77 *"sport is of even greater significance":* Ibid., p. 155.

78 *"contest with himself":* Ibid.

13. ONE GOOD THING

80 *"Stoke Mandeville [is] the only satisfactory unit":* Silver, "Treatment of Spinal Injuries," p. 92.

81 *"to provide an international forum":* Guttmann, "New Hope," p. 1.

82 *"If I ever did one good thing":* Scruton, "Sir Ludwig Guttmann," p. 52.

14. GOING FOR GOLD

85 *"I see people":* Kiger, "Trischa Zorn Inducted."

86 *"As I see it":* International Paralympic Committee, "Franz Nietlispach."

89 *"It was the fastest I'd ever moved":* Lieberman, "Declan Farmer."

90 *"You have the power to be anything":* "About Tatyana."

93 *"I want to show others":* Shriners International, "Brian Bell."

95 *"I feel the same rush":* Davis, phone interview.

SELECTED BIBLIOGRAPHY

"About Tatyana." Tatyana McFadden website. August 2018. http://www.tatyanamcfadden.com./about-tatyana.

Best of Men, The. Written by Lucy Gannon. BBC Television Movie, 2012. DVD.

Brittain, Ian. *From Stoke Mandeville to Stratford: A History of the Summer Paralympic Games.* Champaign, Ill.: Common Ground Publishing, 2012.

Brittain, Ian. *The Paralympic Games Explained.* London and New York: Routledge, 2010.

Buckinghamshire County Council. "History of Spinal Unit at Stoke Mandeville Hospital." Mandeville Legacy: Celebrating Buckinghamshire as the Birthplace of the Paraplegic Movement. November 2017. http://www.mandevillelegacy.org.uk.

Davis, Muffy. Phone interview with Paralympic athlete. March 2018.

Donovan, William H. "Spinal Cord Injury—Past, Present, Future." *Journal of Spinal Cord Medicine* 30, no. 2, 2007, pp. 85–100.

Goodman, Susan. *Spirit of Stoke Mandeville: The Story of Sir Ludwig Guttmann.* London: Collins, 1986. (Based on Guttmann's unfinished autobiography and tapes recorded for the Imperial War Museums.)

Guttmann, Ludwig, and N. C. Mehra. "Experimental Studies on the Value of Archery in Paraplegia." *Spinal Cord* 11, no. 2, 1973, pp. 159–65.

Guttmann, Ludwig. Foreword. *Spinal Cord* 1, no. 1, 1963, p. 1.

Guttmann, Ludwig. "History of the National Spinal Injuries Center, Stoke Mandeville Hospital, Aylesbury." *Spinal Cord* 5, no. 3, 1967, pp. 115–26.

Guttmann, Ludwig. "The Management of the Quinizarin Sweat Test." *Postgraduate Medical Journal* 23, no. 262, 1947, pp. 353–66.

Guttmann, Ludwig. "New Hope for Spinal Cord Sufferers." *Spinal Cord* 17, no. 1, 1979, pp. 6–15.

"Guttmann, Ludwig (Oral History)." Imperial War Museums website, February 28, 2018. http://www.iwm.org.uk/collections/item/object/80004556.

Hughes, J. T. "Historical Review of Paraplegia Before 1918." *Spinal Cord* 25, no. 3, 1987, pp. 168–71.

International Paralympic Committee. "Franz Nietlispach." Official Website of the Paralympic Movement. August 2018. http://www.paralympic.org/athletes/hall-of-fame/inductees-2016.

International Paralympic Committee. "Paralympics—History of the Movement." Official Website of the Paralympic Movement. February 2018. http://www.paralympic.org/the-ipc/history-of-the-movement.

Kiger, Nick. "Trischa Zorn Inducted into Paralympic Hall of Fame." U.S. Paralympics. Team USA website, published by United States Olympic Committee. August 2018. http://www.teamusa.org/US-Paralympics/Features/2012/August/30/Trischa-Zorn-inducted-into-Paralympic-Hall-of-Fame.

"Learn About the Holocaust." United States Holocaust Memorial Museum website. January 2018. http://www.ushmm.org/learn.

Lieberman, Stuart. "Declan Farmer: My First Time." Official Website of the Paralympic Movement. Edited by International Paralympic Committee. August 2018. http://www.paralympic.org/news/declan-farmer-my-first-time.

Mayo Foundation for Medical Education and Research. "Spinal cord injury." Mayo Clinic website. November 2017. http://www.mayoclinic.org/diseases-conditions/spinal-cord-injury/basics/definition/con-20023837.

McDonald, Scott. "Teamwork, Unity Drove Men's Wheelchair Basketball Team to Long-Sought Gold." United States Olympic Committee. Team USA website. September 2018. www.teamusa.org/News/2016/September/23/Teamwork-Unity-Drove-Mens-Wheelchair-Basketball-Team-To-Long-Sought-Gold.

Medawar, J. S., and David Pyke. *Hitler's Gift: The True Story of the Scientists Expelled by the Nazi Regime.* New York: Arcade Publishing, 2012.

Ross, J. Cosbie, and Phillip Harris. "Tribute to Sir Ludwig Guttmann." *Spinal Cord* 18, no. 3, 1980, pp. 153–56.

Scruton, Joan. "Sir Ludwig Guttmann: Creator of a World Sports Movement for the Paralysed and Other Disabled." *Spinal Cord* 17, no. 1, 1979, pp. 52–55.

Shriners International. "Brian Bell Showing No Limits on the Court." September 2018. Shriners International website. http://www.shrinersinternational.org/Press/Corp_Paralympic_Bell.aspx.

Silver, J. R. "History of the Treatment of Spinal Injuries." *Postgrad Medical Journal* 81, no. 952, 2005, pp. 108–14.

Silver, J. R., and M. F. Weiner. "George Riddoch: The Man Who Found Ludwig Guttmann." *Spinal Cord* 50, no. 6, 2012, pp. 88–93.

Whitteridge, David. "Ludwig Guttmann, 3 July 1899–18 March 1980." *Biographical Memoirs of Fellows of the Royal Society* 29, November 1, 1983. Royal Society Publishing, pp. 226–44.

INDEX

Page numbers in *italics* indicate illustrations.

N

O

P

T

U

V

W

Z

PHOTO CREDITS

Cover: MacGregor; Hulton Archive/GETTY
Contents: Raymond Kleboe; Picture Post/GETTY
Epigraph: Keystone; Hulton Archive/GETTY
page 2: Wellcome Collection
page 3: Wikimedia Commons
page 11: FPG / Staff
page 12: KGPA Ltd / Alamy Stock Photo
page 14: Gary Watson/ Science Source
page 17: Barbara Maliszewska; Wikimedia Commons
page 18: Andreas Zerndl; iStock Photos
page 19: Bettmann/GETTY
page 20: Wellcome Collection
page 24: Sueddeutsche Zeitung Photo / Alamy Stock Photo
page 25: U.S. Holocaust Memorial Museum courtesy of Hans Frankl
pages 26, 29, 30: World History Archive / Alamy Stock Photo
page 38: Postgraduate Medical Journal; BMJ Publishing Group Ltd
page 42: Pictorial Press Ltd / Alamy Stock Photo
page 50: Raymond Kleboe / Stringer
page 55: Trinity Mirror / Mirrorpix; Stock Photos/ALAMY
page 64: MacGregor / Stringer
page 65: Bettmann / Contributor
pages 67, 68: WheelPower; Mandeville Legacy
page 71: ©IWAS – www.iwasf.com
page 72, 73: Margaret Maughan; Mandeville Legacy
page 76: Keystone; Hulton Archive/GETTY
page 77: ©the International Paralympic Committee
page 79: Australian Paralympic Committee; Wikimedia Commons
page 82: ©IWAS – www.iwasf.com
page 83: Aflo Co. Ltd. / Alamy Stock Photo
page 84: Aris Messinis/ Stringer
page 87: Gallo Images / Stringer
page 88: Martin Rose / Staff
page 91: PA Images / Alamy Stock Photo
page 92: Friedemann Vogel / Stringer
page 94: Kristan Jacobsen Photography
page 95: Adam Pretty / Staff

ACKNOWLEDGMENTS

Thank you to the following organizations for their assistance with photo research: International Paralympic Committee, International Wheelchair & Amputee Sports Federation, WheelPower, US Holocaust Memorial Museum, and Laura Cotton, Archivist at Buckinghamshire County Council. Thanks to Angeline Carbajal, program coordinator at the University of Arizona, for introducing me to local Paralympic athletes. It was a pleasure and a thrill to speak with gold medal winners Muffy Davis and Jennifer Poist. Thank you to Ann Rider, Kiffin Steurer, Natalie Fondriest, Elizabeth Agyemang, and the rest of the HMH team for helping to make this book the very best it could be. Thanks to Allan Drummond, whose illustrations tie the text and photographs together so beautifully. And a final thank you to Eva Loeffler, who encouraged me to share her father's story with young readers.